Ghosts of W

Other titles in this series include:

HAUNTED BERKSHIRE
Angus Macnaghten

GHOSTS OF EAST ANGLIA
Harold Mills-West

GHOSTS AND FOLKLORE OF NORTHAMPTONSHIRE
Marian Pipe

GHOSTS OF SURREY
John Janaway

LEICESTERSHIRE GHOSTS AND LEGENDS
David Bell

SUSSEX GHOSTS AND LEGENDS
Tony Wales

CHESHIRE GHOSTS AND LEGENDS
Frederick Woods

Ghosts of Warwickshire

Betty Smith

COUNTRYSIDE BOOKS
NEWBURY, BERKSHIRE

First Published 1992

Countryside Books
3 Catherine Road, Newbury, Berkshire

ISBN 1 85306 194 8

Produced through MRM Associates Ltd., Reading
Typeset by Paragon Typesetters, Sandycroft, Chester
Printed by J. W. Arrowsmith Ltd., Bristol

Acknowledgements

I am, as ever, grateful to the staffs of many libraries and record offices for their unfailing help in my research with special thanks to the Shakespeare Trust record office. I am indebted to many people who, over many years, have taken the trouble to write to me with snippets of information for my 'collection', who have told me their own versions of local tales, and who have dredged through their memories to recall legends they learned in their childhood. And my grateful thanks again to my husband, Vic Smith, who helped in my discoveries, sifted, sorted, and read for me.

I am even grateful to my ancient manual typewriter, of impeccable vintage, which has been my friend and 'third hand' for years, and which coughs occasionally, but keeps going.

Contents

Introduction

LET me say at the outset that this book is in no way intended as a serious study of psychic manifestation, but more a simple account of the many ghost stories relative to my native Warwickshire. I cannot vouch for their truth. Ghost belief is as old as mankind, and for centuries such stories have been handed down from one generation to the next, invariably gaining in the re-telling, since long before the Norsemen sat around their fires telling each other sagas. Probably early cavemen communicated such stories to each other in a series of grunts as they gnawed upon their dinosaur steaks! Such tales are an important part of our folklore and should not be lost.

A couple of hundred years or so ago people were not so sceptical, and were more ready to believe in ghosts. Nowadays anything that smacks of the supernatural is seldom discussed for fear of ridicule. This is a pity if it means that our native folklore ceases to be enriched by such traditional stories.

In these days of speed, science and technology, there is less and less likelihood of people accepting that something appearing before them might not have a logical explanation, might just possibly be a 'ghost'. We no longer tell each other stories round the fire. Instead, the central heating is left switched on while we go off to aerobics class or the golf club where the activity is purely physical and readily understandable. Ask anyone if they believe in ghosts – at best they will express a willingness to believe should they personally ever encounter one; at worst, you will get a hoot of satirical laughter.

What is a ghost? This has puzzled many learned people for years. The Ghost Club, founded as long ago as 1862, has undertaken much careful study of psychic phenomena, with controlled experiments set up in various haunted places, and although they have seen and recorded many things, they have still not been able to come up with an absolute and definite answer to this specific question.

Why do ghosts linger here instead of getting on with their proper business in some other world? It used to be thought they remained because of something left undone at their death, which prevented them lying quiet in their graves. The ghost of the murder victim wants vengeance upon the murderer; the suicide buried at the crossroads wants proper burial; the miser wants his hoard to be found. Or they were thought to want to stay on in the place that was especially dear to them in life, and to be near those they cared for.

Ghost legends attached to springs, streams, standing stones, boundary markers and sometimes trees, may well have their origin in pagan times when our ancestors believed these things contained spirits, and venerated them. This type of ghost legend can be found all over the world, and has a germ of logic in that without water, growing things, and boundary markers, the tribe may not survive. Thus the unseen spirits inhabiting these places were revered, placated, and have eventually come down to us as 'ghosts'.

Another puzzling question is why one person can see or feel a 'presence' while a companion standing close by neither sees nor feels anything at all. No one knows, except that some people are more receptive and sensitive to atmosphere than others. Yet ghosts have appeared before even the most hard-bitten, unbelieving and sceptical people, who eventually have to shamefacedly admit there was 'something there' that couldn't be explained away.

I was once told by a friend, who is a respected psychic medium, that everyone is born with psychic perception. Witness small children and their imaginary 'friends'. But this perception is soon erased or eroded by modern civilisation, and the firmly held idea that what you cannot see and prove, scientifically, cannot exist. One of my children had such a friend who often took tea with us. She didn't eat much! And she was offered sweets which she did not accept! With schooldays, she disappeared, but I wish I had known more about her.

At the risk of giving rise to hoots of derision, I hereby admit that I have seen ghosts! What they were, I know not, but I saw them. The image was very like the one you see on a photographic negative when you hold it up to the daylight. I lived for 20 years in a very nice comfortable old house where a little girl appeared on the landing at the top of the stairs at regular intervals. Members of my family and some visitors saw her too. I could not find out who she was, although I did try, but she was dressed in the fashion of a century ago, had long straight hair, brown in colour, and wore a white pinafore. Her presence caused us no upset; in fact we all grew rather fond of her. Twice, though, she took books from their place upstairs and put them in the middle of the floor in the hall downstairs, for some reason best known to herself.

In another house where we lived for nine years, the shade of an elderly man moved along where the kitchen wall is now, but had not used to be. I made enquiries, described the man, and was told by locals that it was an exact description of a former owner of the house, dead long before my time. Apparently, it was his invariable habit to put on his cap at quarter to nine each evening, and head towards the pub, where he had one pint, and one pint only, before he returned home to his bed. It seems he still continues this habit.

There was another much less comfortable occasion when I accompanied my friend, the medium, to observe her at work. The owner of a very old house (not in Warwickshire) was troubled with psychic manifestation, and he asked her to try to find out what it was all about. I was not going to be involved at all, just watch, and I had certainly never set foot in the area before, never seen the house before, nor had I ever met the owner. Neither had my friend!

To my astonishment and discomfiture, I was unwittingly involved the moment I walked through the door. I saw endless pictures flashing with amazing rapidity before my eyes; I heard sounds of voices, and I knew the names of those who spoke. I even knew where the cellar was, although it had been blocked up for more than 50 years. I do not know how I knew!

It totally exhausted me, and every bit of my strength drained away, leaving me so limp my legs could hardly hold me up. When I got back home, I went to bed and slept solidly for 48 hours. My friend was also exhausted, but not as much as me, and she told me later 'You must not let 'them' take so much from you. You should put your guard up . . .' I didn't know what a guard was, nor how to put it up, and I still don't. I have avoided further involvement. I cannot afford the time to sleep for 48 hours on the run. I offer no explanation, for I have none. I am merely telling you what happened.

In discussing the supernatural, allowance must, of course, be made for suggestibility, although I don't see how this could apply to my experience in the old house. The owner had never met either of us before, and as he himself didn't know what had taken place in his house, he would not have been able to project *his* thoughts into my head.

Suggestibility and credulousness do play their part in some stories, though. Lots of things play tricks on the nervous, especially at night. Trees sway, creak and groan; the moon casts inexplicable, odd-shaped shadows; nocturnal creatures squeak and rustle in the undergrowth; domestic animals lurk inside bushes, make noises and exude breath which hangs like vapour on the night air. Even allowing for all of these, there are hundreds of perfectly normal, sane, intelligent people who have witnessed some form of psychic manifestation, something outside of the normal, for which they can find no logical reason. They cannot all be dismissed simply as neurotic and foolish.

The ghosts in this book may or may not be 'real'. They have all been seen by somebody at some time, even though that may have been a very long time ago. The sightings have either been recorded in manuscript form somewhere; alternatively, the legend has been handed down orally, and remains in existence today. I have collected such stories for more than 30 years, and I have visited almost all the places concerned.

The ghosts that abound throughout Warwickshire are legion.

So many are there it is almost more remarkable not to have seen one than otherwise!

At Pillerton Priors, for example, there is a grey lady said to haunt the site of the old church, burned down in 1666. An elderly lady I knew, now dead these many years, and who lived nearby, told me she quite often saw the grey lady, and had always wondered who she was and why she lingered.

The former Council offices at Shipston-on-Stour, once long ago the old Rectory, has a 'something' on the upper floors. Cleaning ladies have been somewhat disturbed in their mopping-up operations by the discovery that they were not alone, and that a shadowy figure wearing headgear rather like a tricorne hat, lurked in the corner. No one knows who it could be.

Again at Shipston-on-Stour there exists a version of the oft-recurring story of the ghost of an old lady, clad in bonnet and shawl, who regularly appeared at a crossroads. When this particular piece of road had eventually to be dug up, as all roads do from time to time, female bones were discovered, and there was the vague and unsubstantiated suggestion of a stake through the heart. It was, therefore, decided that the old lady had either taken her own life, or been suspected of witchcraft, and had been buried at the crossroads without benefit of clergy. The bones were given burial and she has not appeared since. Similar legends exist in many villages, located at either a crossroads where traditionally suicides or those dabbling in the black arts were buried, that all might walk over them; at other times the location is near a spring or a well, or a parish boundary stone.

There are many stories of witches in Warwickshire, all of whom seem to have come to a bad end, and refused to lie quiet. It is slightly disconcerting to find that most of them were called 'Betty'.

The Tredington 'Betty' is to be seen sitting on the church-yard wall, smoking a pipe! She made her modest living by threatening to put spells on everyone who refused her food and firing. But she played fair, and only took what she wanted for her immediate needs.

There are similar stories of witch ghosts at Loxley and at Walcot, both of whom seem to have been very vengeful and had the enviable ability to turn themselves into hares, the better to get around and work their evil will without being spotted. One night, Betty the witch of Loxley in her hare disguise, was shot by a poacher, and the following day was seen to have a wounded arm!

At Ilmington there is a 'Betty's Well' called after the old witch who lived in a cottage nearby, and who still makes disconcerting noises around the spot at night.

Monks we have in plenty. The ghost of a grey-cowled brother haunts the road running between the villages of Oxhill and Whatcote at a spot where a small stream forms a parish boundary, and where a gate once hung when this route was but a muddy track. It is thought that the inn at Whatcote, the Royal Oak, was built by the monks of Bordesley Abbey which owned land here, some 800 years ago. It was used as one of their retreat houses, and the ghost monk may be of that period.

Another monkish figure flits around at Alderminster. There was a convent here way back in the 5th century, but there has never been a monastery. However, the village was completely wiped out by the Black Death in 1349, and it is thought the ghost could be that of an itinerant friar passing through who stayed to help minister to the sick, and succumbed to the dread disease himself.

The old manor house at Clifford Chambers, just outside Stratford-upon-Avon was once a monastic stopping place, literally the 'chambers' where the Abbot stayed when he was doing his rounds! At the Dissolution, one old Abbot flatly refused to budge, and he went further, putting a curse upon all who might live in that house. He stayed there until 1918 when the manor house was rebuilt, and legend has it that a Bible was built into the wall of what had been the Abbot's room, and this has kept him quiet ever since.

At Brailes, the lovely little Catholic church is hidden well away inside a farmhouse. It was contrived from an old malt barn in the days of intensive religious persecution, and is said to be haunted by the ghost of a nun. Legend has it that she secretly gave birth to a child, and because of the great scandal attached to this confirmation of an illicit relationship, the infant was taken from her. She has been searching for it ever since.

At Salford Hall, Salford Priors, now a prestigious hotel, there is the ghost of a benign and gentle grey-clad nun, left over from when the hall was the home of Benedictine nuns who fled from the ravages of the French Revolution.

There are quite a few phantom coaches hurtling about the county, some drawn by headless horses, others driven by headless drivers, but Bedworth goes one better, and has a phantom funeral. This was well reported in the 1920s and those who saw it said the horses were black, with black plumes on their heads, and the hearse and its trappings were of the late Victorian period. The cortege entered Wootton Street in the doubtful light of winter mornings, and moving slowly, made its way along the length of the street to disappear at the other end. Although the funeral procession did not alter its steady pace, no one was able to catch up with it, or even get near to it.

We have a few white ladies too. One is said to glide up and down the staircase at Ettington Park, once the home of the Shirley family, but now a hotel for many years. This extraordinary Gothic building was built last century to replace a much earlier and much more beautiful house on the same site. Used as a location for several films, the present building presents a somewhat eerie facade, particularly when the mist rises gently from the lake in front of it. No one knows who the white lady is, nor has she been dated.

Another white-clad female is said to haunt the bank of a small stream at Wellesbourne, where legend has it she drowned herself. Preston Bagot had a white lady flitting about the churchyard, although there is no true description of this apparition on record. However, during necessary repairs to the church, two skeletons were found between the inner and outer walls. These were buried, and no one has seen the white lady since.

Just for a change, there is a ghost cyclist at Stoneleigh. Dressed in the knickerbockers of the late Victorian era, he rides a large 'sit-up-and-beg' bicycle, careers wildly down the hill and fails to negotiate the bend at the bottom. The cycle crashes into the parapet of the bridge that crosses the river there. This did in fact happen sometime during the 1880s when Stoneleigh was a Sunday excursion for cyclists from Coventry. The accident proved fatal to this poor young man, whose name is not known.

The population of Warwickshire, like all other counties, has changed dramatically over the past decade. It has become much more transient. Motorways have materialised, and these have lead to more development. Places and landscapes are changed beyond recognition, and it is now virtually impossible to discover an 'old inhabitant' who can tell you a ghost story of their village from first hand experience. But still, newcomers learn the legends of the place where they have made their new home, and thus are the stories perpetuated, but for how long remains to be seen!

Usually, the finer details are long gone. In the interests of readability, I have reconstructed the bare bones of a flimsy legend into a story. These are not by any means all the ghost stories of Warwickshire, but I rather fancy they are a reasonably good cross-section of the wealth of our folklore.

Whether you believe in ghosts or not does not matter. Read them simply as stories; stories which form threads in the great tapestry that gives us a picture of the life, events, beliefs and superstitions of this county over many hundreds of years. I hope you will enjoy them.

Betty Smith
September 1992

Select Bibliography

Shakespeare Land (C J Ribton-Turner 1893)
Rambles in Shakespeare's Country (J H Wade 1932)
Warwickshire (J Lisle 1936)
Bygone Warwickshire (W Andrews 1893)
Historic Warwickshire (J T Burgess 1893)
Warwickshire (D Hickman 1979)
Warwickshire Villages (L F Cave 1976)
Folklore of Warwickshire (R Palmer 1976)
Short History of Warwickshire and Birmingham (V Bird 1977)
Tiddyoody Pie (F W Bennett 1930)
Highways and Byways in Shakespeare Country (W H Hutton 1914)
Folklore, Old Customs and Superstitions in Shakespeareland (J H Bloom 1929)
Warwickshire (C Holland 1906)
Rural Romance (T Horniblow 1923)
Shakespeare's Greenwood (G Morley 1900)
Edgehill 1642 (P Young 1967)
Haunted Warwickshire (M E Atkins 1981)
Warwickshire (W Smith 1830)
Warwickshire (A Mee 1936)
Haunted England (C Hole 1940)
Rambles Round the Edgehills (G Miller 1967)
Rosemary for Stratford (U Bloom 1966)
Parson Extraordinary (U Bloom)
Warwickshire(A Burgess 1950)
Unknown Warwickshire (Dormer Harris 1924)
Summer Days in Shakespeareland (C Harper 1912)
Poems of Warwickshire, An Anthology (Ed. R Pringle 1980)
Through the Lychgate (E Rainsberry 1969)
Newspapers and magazines: The Stratford-upon-Avon Herald; The Leamington Spa Courier; Warwick Advertiser; Evesham Journal; Coventry Evening Telegraph; Nuneaton Newspapers. Focus magazine; Warwickshire County Magazine; Warwickshire and Worcestershire Life etc.
Notes and transactions of many societies now extinct, plus hundreds of church and village booklets, gathered over many years, of which I now have an enormous collection.

1

Ghosts of Warwick Castle

THE great fortress of Warwick Castle stands in the centre of the county town, lodged firmly on a mound created by Ethelfleda, the war-like daughter of King Alfred the Great. After the Norman invasion, William the Conqueror gave Warwick to one of his most loyal followers, Henry de Newburgh, who became the first Earl of Warwick. He removed the modest wooden structure left by Turchil the Saxon, and after the fashion of the Normans built himself a castle of stone.

It has withstood the storms and tempests of nine centuries, and each successive earl has left his mark upon it. Within its massive walls, rising sheer and cliff-like above the river, all the great figures whose names appear in school history books have stayed, slept, fought, argued and loved.

Here in 1266 Henry III made his plans for the Siege of Kenilworth; here they dragged Piers Gaveston for his travesty of a trial; the weak and foolish King Edward II was brought to Warwick under pressure to sign away the throne of his father; here came Henry V after Agincourt, and Richard Neville, the 'Kingmaker', brought Edward IV here as his prisoner in 1469.

It is strange to think that none of these colourful and charismatic figures have left any shade behind them. The ghost of Warwick Castle is of a much softer mould.

When Sir Fulke Greville received the castle from James I in 1605 it was in a very ruinous state, and he immediately set about restoring it, and turning it from a bleak fortress into a civilised home. He spent £30,000 upon it, and that was a considerable fortune in those days, but he did have a considerable fortune, for he was descended from that family of Greville who became very rich indeed in the thriving days of the wool trade.

Fulke Greville was born at Beauchamp Court, near Alcester, in 1554. A learned, scholarly and much travelled man, he was knighted in 1597, and created Baron in 1620. He was the faithful servant of Queen Elizabeth I, and the confidant of James I, who stayed with him at Warwick Castle in 1617, 1619, 1621, and 1624. Greville is said to have been the most witty and generous of hosts, and the English poet Bishop Richard Corbet, another regular visitor, said of him that his 'every word was wine and musick'. Greville wrote over 100 sonnets, and two tragedies, notably the 'Tragedy of Mustapha'. His 'Life' of his friend Sidney was published in 1652.

Greville's end was a sad and unwarranted finale to an exemplary life which is perhaps why he lingers still. It was on 30th September 1628, when he was 74 years of age, and was staying for a while at his London home, Brooke House. He was apparently preparing his last will and testament, sitting at a small table writing. He called for his manservant, Hayward, an elderly man who had been long in his service, and when Hayward answered his master's summons, Greville told him to witness his signature to the document on the table before him. Hayward did as he was bidden.

When Greville's attention was briefly turned elsewhere, Hayward seized the opportunity to look at the paper he had just signed, and recognised it as Sir Fulke's will. Hastily he skimmed down the page, and with chagrin realised his name did not appear. After many years of faithful service, his master had bequeathed him nothing. This was not what he had been led to expect. He had thought he would receive some reward.

To be cast off without a penny after all he had done! Rage mounted in Hayward's breast, and when Sir Fulke sat down again at the writing table, Hayward took a knife and stabbed him in the back. With scarcely a groan Sir Fulke Greville fell dead across the table.

Hayward looked down at his dead master; at the rapidly widening pool of blood, the result of the crime he had just committed, and he was overcome with terror, as well he might be. Then, according to Dugdale, he 'went into another room and having lock't the door, pierced his own bowels with a sword . . .' Thus did the murderer die with his victim.

Sir Fulke's body was brought back to Warwick for burial, and was laid out in the Water Gate Tower, in the suite of rooms he always used for his own when in residence. There it remained for several days that all might pay their proper respects to him.

Sir Fulke lies buried in St Mary's church, Warwick, alongside all the other great earls in their sumptuous and magnificent tombs. Upon that of Sir Fulke there is no effigy, but a painting of him as a young man hangs in his room in the castle. It is from behind this portrait that his ghost appears, quite gentle, but sad. It is almost as if he had no wish to leave the castle he had restored with such pride, and which he was known to love. The ghost has been seen by many people, and there was a time when cleaners became so apprehensive, they refused to deal with this particular room.

Another famous ghost of the castle was considerably more boisterous and much more of a nuisance in her day, although it is not absolutely clear which era was 'her day'.

Standing in the street and looking across the river to the rising castle walls, you may be able to discern a stone figure, much battered now by wind and weather. This is a 'watcher' put there by stonemasons of old and intended to fool any possible enemy sauntering about below into believing they were being watched. It is also said to mark the spot where Moll Bloxham, the witch, jumped into the river.

According to the legend, Moll was a servant of the castle, and when she grew too old to carry out her duties as rigorously as might be expected, she was given leave to remain, staying in a small 'attic' room. She was also given permission to take surplus butter, milk and eggs from the castle kitchens, and sell them to the townsfolk. She made a very good thing out of this 'franchise' and was able to put quite a few coins under her mattress. But like many people, Moll got greedy. Not content with getting a reasonable price for the butter, milk and eggs, which cost her nothing at all, she kept on putting her prices up. With her reputation for possibly dabbling in the black arts, the local people were wary of her, and had no recourse but to pay the price she demanded.

Eventually Moll's prices became so high, there were rumblings among the populace, and they officially complained to the Earl of the time that they were being systematically cheated. This was the first the Earl had heard of it, but he took immediate steps and gave instructions that Moll was to receive no more supplies from his kitchens. Her privilege was withdrawn forthwith.

Moll retired to her own tiny room and set about revenge, using her powers of witchcraft. She was not seen wandering through the multitudinous passages of the castle any more. Instead, she turned herself into a great black hound, and this creature roamed through the passages instead, howling, snarling and frightening all and sundry.

No one could get near the hound, or catch it, and in any case, knowing it was really Moll Bloxham, they were too afraid to try. But at length it could be tolerated no longer, and the Earl summoned three clergymen to the castle to do something about it.

The three clergymen were probably just as terrified as everybody else, but the great Earl had told them to 'do something' and so they must needs obey.

They formed a plan to trap the creature in some small room at the top of the castle, and then read the service of exorcism. They couldn't think of anything else that might serve!

They chased the beast. It was huge, much bigger than any ordinary hound. It lead them a merry dance, every now and again turning to glare at them with its red eyes, its teeth bared and slavering. But the intrepid clergymen persevered, and eventually cornered the creature. They approached, starting to intone the prayers of the exorcism, when suddenly the hound gave a great leap, over the walls and into the river below. The clergymen watched its descent, and noted that when it was about half way down the great drop, the hound was a hound no longer, but had turned itself back into the old woman, Moll Bloxham.

To this very day, the story goes, the evil spirit of the old woman, and her bones, lie trapped, imprisoned beneath the stones of the weir below the castle walls. The black hound was never seen again.

2

The Ladies and the Cleric

CLOPTON House stands amid modest parkland a mile or so outside the town of Stratford-upon-Avon, and has the reputation of being the most haunted house in the Midlands. So many ghosts flit about within its venerable walls that one might be forgiven for wondering if there remains any room for living people!

There have been Cloptons living in a house on this site since around 1220. The family were never especially notable in the annals of the history of England, but nevertheless they fulfilled a useful role locally and played their part in that station of life into which they were born. Clopton House has gone through many vicissitudes, and at several times throughout the centuries, has fallen into dereliction and decay.

It has had many lively owners. One, Charles Warde, completely rebuilt the house in 1846 and proceeded to embark upon a life so riotous and so dissipated that he was finally disgraced, bankrupt and banished, having earned for himself the nickname 'Warwickshire Casanova'. Writer and essayist William Howitt visited in 1840 and declared 'Clopton must have been in its dereliction just the place for fermenting tales of superstition'. Thus have many stories and legends grown up around the old place.

The three 'main' ghosts, if indeed any ghost is more 'main' than another, are three Clopton daughters who appear to have been singularly ill-fated, and who still linger in the house that was their home.

In 1546, a dread visitor came to Stratford-upon-Avon. The

Plague was carried thither by Lord Leicester's soldiers returning from war in the Low Countries. It was not long before the fearsome disease roared through the town like a fire carrying all before it. Many people fled into the surrounding countryside, but very few within the town escaped, and the plague exacted its toll of victims, rich and poor alike.

Charlotte Clopton, described as frail and delicate, was an all too easy prey, but her sorrowing family had scant time for their grief. It was necessary to get the bodies of the dead below ground as quickly as possible in a vain bid to halt the spread of the pestilence. Charlotte was hastily put into a plain coffin and interred at dead of night in the Clopton vault in Holy Trinity church.

Within three weeks, the Clopton family were once again plunged into sorrow, for Charlotte's mother who had devotedly nursed her daughter, succumbed and died, her end doubtless hastened by her grief. Again, the Cloptons hastily prepared her body for burial at dead of night. Again, the dark trek to Holy Trinity church, and the opening of the Clopton tomb.

But when the vault was opened, the mourners stood transfixed with horror at what was revealed to them. In seeking to lay poor Lady Clopton reverently to her last rest, they discovered that her daughter, Charlotte, had not been laid to rest at all. Charlotte had not been dead at the time of her burial, and she was found leaning against the wall inside the vault. It is presumed that she had awakened from her death-like coma, and with the strength of sheer terror, had broken free of her coffin, but had not been able to free herself from the stone vault. She had eventually died, standing up, leaning against the wall. Her hands were torn and bloody from her frenzied efforts and the stones were stained in places where her small frail hands had frantically clawed at them. Even more terrifying to those who looked inside, Charlotte Clopton, in her final death agonies, had begun to eat her own forearm.

Charlotte was reverently and properly buried again, close to her mother, but her slim shadow returned to Clopton House to wander sadly through the room where she died.

Mrs Gaskell, when a young girl at school in Stratford-upon-Avon, visited Clopton House in the 1820s, and later wrote of a 'pent-up atmosphere and eerie feeling' in one of the bedrooms, where hung a portrait that was 'singularly beautiful'. Elizabeth Gaskell described the portrait as that of a sweet looking girl with pale gold hair falling into ringlets upon her neck and eyes like 'violets filled with dew'. This, she said, was Charlotte Clopton, and this was the room wherein she still walks.

Another daughter of the house who met a tragic end was Margaret Clopton.

Margaret had the misfortune to fall deeply and passionately in love with a young man whom her family considered totally unsuitable as a husband for her. Since in 1588 daughters were jealously guarded by their parents and their daily lives greatly circumscribed, we do not know how or where Margaret met this young man. Margaret's father, Sir William, entertained higher hopes for his daughter than a penniless youth with no prospects and no lineage, and he forbade the association.

Margaret was forbidden to leave the house. Poor unhappy Margaret pined, wept and pleaded for her young lover, but to no avail. Sir William remained adamant.

Doubtless Sir William believed he was doing his best for his much loved daughter, but Margaret would not be consoled. She locked herself in her room, refused to eat or speak, and her health and spirits went into a 'decline'. Perhaps the household thought 'leave her alone and she'll come round' was the best policy, but it did not work this time. In the best tradition of all such heroines, desperately suffering the pangs of unrequited love, Margaret crept from her self-inflicted imprisonment one balmy summer night. Silently she stole down the back stairs while the household slept, and making her way to the end of the garden, she drowned herself in the well. There she was discovered the following morning, her long hair floating on the surface of the petal strewn water. Her body, enwrapped in its sodden garments, was lifted from the well but her wraith had already returned to remain forever in the room where Margaret spent her last unhappy days.

Alice Clopton too haunts the upper rooms of her old home, but since her story is largely legendary, her dates are not known.

Alice Clopton was betrothed and about to be married. Happily Alice had fallen in love with a young man who was considered very suitable to be her husband, and everyone looked favourably upon the match. The date for the wedding was fixed upon, and doubtless, the young Alice was busy preparing her gown, gathering her trousseau, and learning household management from her mother. But dire fate took a hand, and Alice's happiness was all too short-lived.

There was another young man who declared himself to be in love with Alice, and said no one else should have her. He was a very unsuitable suitor. Alice wanted none of him, and her parents believed he was more in love with Alice's inheritance and her dowry than with Alice herself. The young man did not take his refusal graciously and warned the Cloptons they had not heard the last of him.

It was on the eve of Alice's wedding day that he again made his appearance. He had kept watch upon the house, and espying Alice alone in the garden, he rode up with a great flourish, grabbed her unceremoniously, and flung her across his saddle. Alice screamed, and servants and family came running just in time to see the abductor galloping furiously off in the direction of the small village of Birmingham.

Alice's betrothed, her father and retainers hastily mounted and set off in hot pursuit. The abductor forced his horse to an even greater speed, still keeping a cruel hold upon the screaming and terrified Alice.

It was not until he was approaching Birmingham that he realised the pursuers were gaining upon him. Their hoof beats were getting closer and he could see them not all that far behind him. His horse, having been hard driven, was tiring, and Alice's screams and struggles were hampering him. He rode on to a small rough bridge at Deritend, straggling the river Rae, and without more ado, he flung Alice from him, over the bridge and into the murky waters below. He did not pause, but his horse, its burden lightened, was forced into another burst of speed, and the cowardly abductor made his escape.

Alice's betrothed leapt from his horse and rushed to the aid of the luckless Alice, but he was too late. Poor terrified Alice was drowned, and as he lifted her body from the water, the young man vowed he would never marry, but would remain a hermit for the rest of his life.

This sacred and knightly vow he kept. He took up his abode in a cave within rocks overlooking the river Severn, where he rapidly gained the reputation of being one of 'the Wise Ones'. People came from far and wide to consult him upon many matters, and he lived upon food left for him at his doorstep.

One day, many years on, a man entered the cave and Alice's betrothed, now older, unkempt and with a long beard, instantly recognised his visitor as the man who had abducted and killed the girl who was to have become his wife.

It was too much for him. He gave a piercing shriek and flung himself upon the man. Locked together, they crashed on to the rocks in the river below, where they both perished.

The three ladies flitting forlornly through the upper rooms at Clopton House also have ecclesiastical company. The ghost is the unquiet wraith of a priest, foully murdered whilst at prayer in a secret chapel at the top of the house. The story has it that the stains of his blood upon its floor could never be removed.

Little detail is known about the end of this unfortunate cleric. The Clopton family were Catholic, and in the times of religious persecution, they, like many other such families, had a hidden chapel, and sheltered visiting priests. However, one former owner, the late Lady Utica Beecham, who occasionally showed people around her home, was wont to point to the staining, and tell the story that it was a priest involved in the Gunpowder Plot, for Clopton House had a role to play in this colourful episode in history.

In 1604 Clopton House came into the hands of George Carew (pronounced 'Carey') through his marriage with Joyce Clopton. Carew (later created Baron Clopton) was a staunch Protestant, son of the Dean of Windsor. Whether he knew of the secret chapel is not recorded. He was in no hurry to come to Clopton House, and it remained empty for some time, with a man called Robert Willson left in charge of the property on a kind of caretaking arrangement.

Willson was approached by a man called Ambrose Rokewood, who suggested he might rent the house for a short time. Willson, quite properly, replied that he would need to consult his absent master on this matter, but Rokewood told him he need have no fear. Carew was a friend of his, he said, and he was absolutely certain that he would agree to the arrangement. After all, it was for but a short time. Almost before Willson could blink an eye, Rokewood with two friends, Grant and Wyntor, had moved 'their stuffes' into the house and settled themselves.

It is extremely unlikely that Carew would ever have agreed to this had he known of it. And it is extremely unlikely that he numbered Rokewood among his friends.

Rokewood, Grant and Wyntor were, of course, conspirators in the notorious Gunpowder Plot. Their fellow conspirators had taken up residence all around the area, and organised hunting expeditions enabling them all to meet together regularly in the most innocent of circumstances. Rokewood was right when he said it would only be for a short time. Their plans were laid, and all they had to do now was to await news of the success of their plotting.

The Gunpowder Plot, as we know, failed dismally, and when the news reached Warwickshire, Rokewood and the others fled from Clopton House to be eventually captured just over the border into Worcestershire.

Clopton House, together with many other houses belonging to Catholic families, was raided by armed men, who found their birds flown. At Clopton, however, they discovered the secret chapel and its 'massing reliques' which they took away with them.

It is known that many of the conspirators had priests with them to enable them to hear the Mass. Perhaps the cleric who walks the upper storey of Clopton House was one of these.

After the trial of the Gunpowder conspirators, George Carew found it expedient to carry out some repairs and restorations to the old house. But he did not remove the chapel. It became known as the 'text room' because of the texts painted upon its walls, but was never again used for worship. Except perhaps by the ghostly cleric!

Eventually the house became the home of Sir Arthur Hodgson who made a great fortune in Australia, and decided to return to his native hearth to play the part of squire. He openly refuted any idea that Clopton House was haunted, and laughed to scorn all the tales connected with it. But he did eventually admit that he had once put a guest to sleep in the Priest's Chamber. The guest departed hurriedly the following morning, declaring nothing would induce him to remain another night in the house.

Clopton House still stands, but much altered. In 1982 the remaining contents were sold at public auction, and the house itself was bought by developers, who have turned it into luxurious apartments. Margaret's well is still there. But whether Charlotte, Margaret, Alice and the priest have ever manifested themselves to the new residents we may never know.

3

The Monks who Moved House

FILLONGLEY lies to the west of Coventry, and whilst it still struggles to retain its identity, the advent of modern development and motorways has marred its once peaceful charm. It is probably the only village in the county that once had two castles, but Oliver Cromwell put paid to both of them and little remains now but traces of the mounds upon which they stood.

The venerable Church of St Mary and All Saints dates back to the 13th century, the list of the clergy serving it beginning in 1248. But it is not clergy that haunt this lovely old building, it is a group of monks who have no rightful business there at all.

There have been many sightings of cowled figures, accompanied by the sound of the Latin chant. Earlier this century, local people complained that when they walked down the path to the church to attend services, they felt as if they were being held back by an invisible force, almost as if someone was standing in front of them, barring their way and pushing against them.

Back in the dark days of the Second World War, the wife of the vicar at that time was going into the church on some minor parish business. It was just getting dark, and as she hurried inside, she saw movement, and to her astonishment, she saw a man in what she took to be a black cassock standing near the altar. Not unnaturally, she thought it was her husband, and was at a loss to understand how he had got here, since she had only just left him at home, sitting by the war-rationed fire, comfortably clad in his cardigan and carpet slippers. She went towards him, and called his name, when quite suddenly the black clad figure simply dissolved. There was no one there at all.

Stories of hauntings and tales of the supernatural flew thick and fast about Fillongley at one stage, and one very down-to-earth, exceedingly sceptical gentleman decided enough was enough. He didn't believe in ghosts, and he scoffed openly at those who declared they had witnessed psychic manifestation of any kind. He was going to lay this silly story for good and all, he said, before the entire village got caught up in supernatural fever. He was going to spend an entire night alone in the church, and prove to everyone that it was all a load of rubbish!

He marched fearlessly into the church as darkness was closing in, and just after midnight he left it again, at a run! He was plainly frightened and ashen faced, but refused to say anything. Nothing would induce him to tell his own story, not then and not ever. According to local legend, he never went near the church again for any reason whatsoever.

Since Fillongley never had a monastery, or any resident monks to speak of, it was difficult to comprehend why a group of monks haunted the church. It was eventually discovered that the altar stone in Fillongley church had been brought there from Maxstoke Priory, just a few miles away, and it was decided that the ghost monks had accompanied it.

Maxstoke Priory was founded in 1331 by Sir William de Clinton. There was to be a prior, and twelve canons, all wearing the black cappa and cowl, with white linen such as befitted their station in the hierarchy. They were to have meat and drink, as much bread and ale as they wanted, candles, firing, servants to wait upon them, a new gown each year, and wages too! It seems they were on to a good thing.

It is recorded that they did not live the life of piety usually associated with monasteries, but all had a jolly good roistering time instead, denying themselves nothing. They had jesters to amuse them, troupes of visiting play actors, jugglers and tumblers, singers, and a 'necromancer playing in a painted chamber'. They were a somewhat riotous crew, and there were many official complaints against them for assault and marauding. They were not averse to a spot of theft, and in 1399 one of the brothers murdered one of his fellows.

By the time of the Dissolution in 1536, only seven monks remained at Maxstoke Priory, but they had 26 servants to attend them. These seven were turned out into the hard, cold world, to fend for themselves as best they might, and Maxstoke Priory, which must have been a truly beautiful place, slowly and inexorably fell into ruins. Presumably, the altar stone was ultimately rescued from the ruins and brought into use at Fillongley, but just when, and by whom, is not known. It may also be assumed that the last seven monks died in the fullness of time, and their spirits returned to Maxstoke, a place where they had obviously lived very well indeed. Maybe so well that they were denied a quiet grave. All unwittingly, those who brought the stone also brought the 'Magnificent Seven' who promptly took over Fillongley church, and did their level best to keep everyone else out.

When the reputed hauntings were at the height of their nuisance, one clergyman, whose name is not known to us, volunteered to go into Fillongley church at midnight, and read a specially prepared form of Divine Service designed to quieten even the most troublesome spirit.

This he did, and alone, inside the church, he read the service in Latin. About half way through, he became aware of voices other than his own, joining in, and realised the seven monks were making the correct Latin responses, and actually taking part in the service that was supposed to exorcise their very presence. Not surprisingly, the clergyman did not stay to complete his task, but fled willy-nilly. Presumably, the monks had the last laugh!

If the seven monks who remained there at the Dissolution in 1536 followed their altar stone to Fillongley, it can only be assumed that the ghosts remaining at Maxstoke must be of monks of an earlier period. In the 300 years the priory was in use, many monks must have entered through its handsome gateway, and many others departed, wrapped in cerecloth. These perhaps are the ones who stayed.

Not much remains of Maxstoke Priory now, except some rather lovely arches and gateways. The ruins have become incorporated into a busy working farm, and where the monks once trod, cattle graze. But it is still said the voices of monks may be heard, and their presence felt.

Author Alan Burgess, writing in the 1950s, tells of the time he visited Maxstoke ruins with his younger sister. Together they looked out across the peaceful Warwickshire countryside, and all was serene. Then they too heard the sound of shuffling figures, and the monkish chant in Latin, coming from behind them. They hastily left, and Burgess relates this was the one and only time in his whole life when he actually saw and heard ghosts.

4

Jeremiah Stone and the Devil

JEREMIAH Stone, who came from no one knows quite where, was a Corporal of Dragoons, and fought at Edgehill. In company with many of his fellows, he was wounded, and lay upon the battlefield until dark, but when many of the injured began to stumble and shuffle their way off the field, Jeremiah Stone lingered. He was crafty, and he'd had quite enough of this blooody war already. He was intent upon making off, and he didn't intend to go away empty handed.

His wound was not a severe one, and under cover of darkness he crept stealthily about the field, searching the bodies of the dead for money and valuables. He got quite a good haul, and put it all together in a leather bag which he fastened about his waist. He felt it would probably make his life more comfortable for some time to come, if only he could get away, a long way away. But he had no idea how far he could walk, with the painful wound in his leg, and he felt considerably weakened from loss of blood. He knew he couldn't stay around the battlefield, where he would be absolutely certain to be picked up, so with somewhat faltering steps, he turned his face in the direction of Warwick. The journey took him a long time, for he could make only slow progress, and at the slightest sound, he hid himself behind the hedge, or crouched down in the ditch, but always he kept his hand upon his leather bag of ill-gotten gains.

It was the following day when he arrived in Warwick, and he made for the Anchor Inn, where he explained to the landlord that he was wounded and sorely in need of a bed where he could rest up for a few days until he was strong enough to continue on his way. He was given an upper chamber where he put himself to bed and dozed fitfully. The leather bag he kept under his hand.

When morning came, he realised his wound was much worse, and he couldn't get out of bed. The landlady was very kind to him, and offered to dress his wound and look after him until he was better. He was grateful for this, and securing his leather bag, he asked her if she would keep it somewhere safe for him. He would collect it as soon as he was well, he said, and she would be well paid for her trouble and kindness.

The landlady took the bag and promised to keep it safe, but when she told her husband, and they opened the bag, they immediately tumbled to what had happened. The old leather bag contained far more than a corporal could have amassed by proper means, and where else would he have got jewellery and gold coins except by robbing the dead?

The landlady nursed Jeremiah Stone, who spent several days in fever and delirium, but eventually he regained his strength and decided it was time for him to be on his way. He told the landlady 'I shall be ready to leave today. Please give me back the leather bag that I entrusted to your care.'

The landlady expressed astonishment. 'What leather bag?' she asked. 'You gave no leather bag into my care. And you owe for your food and lodging.'

Jeremiah Stone was incensed. He knew he had been in a fever, but he also knew with absolute certainty that the landlady had taken the bag from him and promised to keep it safe. He got into a violent temper, and verbally attacked the host of the Anchor Inn, calling him and his wife thieves and robbers and much else besides. They decided not to press for the food and lodging money, but instead grabbed Jeremiah Stone by the back of his coat, and physically flung him outside into the street, telling him not to return or they would have the law on him.

There wasn't much Jeremiah could do about it. He had himself stolen the contents of the leather bag, and if he went to the law and protested that it had been stolen from him, there would be a great many awkward questions. Besides, he was a deserter, and was unknown here in Warwick, whereas the landlord and landlady of the Anchor Inn were respectable local people. But he was determined he wouldn't let the matter rest there. He'd get the bag back by fair means or foul!

He lurked about the town until near midnight, and then stealthily returned to the Anchor Inn. It was all locked up, its last topers gone home. Jeremiah Stone, keeping as quiet as possible, broke open a window and began to ease himself inside the inn, where he intended to find his leather bag, and remove it and himself while the household lay abed. But the landlord and landlady expected this and were ready for him. They grabbed him, and pulled him inside through the broken window. He was arrested and charged with breaking and entering before being flung into Warwick gaol to await the next Assizes.

No one believed Stone's story. It was all together too far fetched, and besides everyone knew the Anchor Inn was an honest house. Jeremiah's luck had run out, it seems, and as he festered in the noisome underground cell, he vowed vengeance upon the Anchor Inn.

One night, in the gaol, the Devil appeared before Jeremiah Stone, as in a dream. Indeed, Jeremiah could not ever be certain whether it was a dream or not. But there was the Devil, and he grinned at the luckless Jeremiah. He suggested to him that he would take care of everything, if, in return, he could have Jeremiah's soul. But Stone was not that far removed from reason, and he refused to sell his soul to the Devil.

The Devil took his refusal philosophically. He'd had refusals before, but he pointed out to the miserable man in the cell that he would surely need some help to get him out of his present mess.

'You need someone to speak for you' said the wily old Devil. Stone knew this was true.

'Tell you what,' went on the Devil, 'when you get into court, ask for someone who will speak on your behalf. Tell them you insist upon it as a right, and then look around the court. You will see a man wearing a red hat with a feather in it. Ask that he may be appointed to speak for you.'

The Devil disappeared, and Stone was once more alone in his cell. A very few days later, he was standing in the dock, and he realised only too well how black things looked for him. He remembered what the Devil had told him, and asked if he could have someone to speak for him. The judge agreed, and Stone looked around the courtroom. Spotting a dark-visaged man in a red hat with a feather, he chose him.

The Devil, for he it was wearing the red hat with a feather, told Stone's story to the court, and suggested that the truth of it could easily be proved if a search was immediately made at the Anchor Inn, where he declared the leather bag would be found, hidden by the landlord and landlady who had indeed stolen it.

At hearing this, the landlord of the Anchor Inn jumped to his feet, and with an oath shouted 'This is not true. May the Devil take me if I have ever had any such bag!'

Whereupon the dark-visaged man in the red hat gave a whoop of joy, and re-assuming his devilish guise, he grabbed the landlord, and flew with him, out of the courtroom, right up into the air, where they hovered over the market place, before they finally disappeared, leaving behind them, according to passers-by 'a very grate stinke'.

Thus, occasionally, above the market place in Warwick, the struggling ghost of the landlord, grasped in the iron hands of the Devil, may be faintly discerned floating over the rooftops, with a 'very grate stinke'.

This extraordinary story was reported in a pamphlet dated 1642, printed in London. In it, one John Finch, a 'shoomaker' says he 'doth testify to its truth, being an eye-witness of same'.

5

The Maid of the Common

THIS may be a true story, or it may not! I suspect that like many such tales, handed down from one generation to another, there is a germ of truth buried deep within, and the re-telling has invested it with a romantic aura, as invariably happens. I first heard of it many years ago, and kept a note of it. It has been impossible to check up on it; the names of the protagonists are lost in the mists of time, their ends unknown. But it is too good a story to lose!

It seems there was once a young girl who lived with her mother in a tumbledown hovel on the wastes of Yarningale Common, lying between the villages of Claverdon and Preston Bagot. They were poor, but the girl was not cast in the usual mould of such daughters, for she was beautiful. Not only was she beautiful, but she was a laughing, sparkling, blithe maid, with a form and figure as light as a will o' the wisp. Not surprising then that all the lads of the neighbourhood lingered about Yarningale Common, despite its reputation, for its very name means 'grave of the stranger' and everyone knew that the mound on the common was where ancient tribal chiefs lay buried. But they all risked it just to catch a glimpse of those bright eyes and dainty form. She flirted with them all, but none could hold her until there eventually came one with whom she fell in love, and he with her.

He was a good man if somewhat unimaginative, and of a stolid disposition. He was poor too, and lived with his father in a wooden hut on the canal side at Preston Bagot, where they both earned their living making wooden gates and fences. He wanted to marry the girl. She was willing, but set conditions upon their marriage. She wanted a new life, pretty things and the money to buy them. She would only agree to marry him if he left the wooden hut and went to the town of Birmingham, where he could find well paid work with a joiner. They could leave the bleak countryside and live a more lively life in the town.

The young man didn't want this at all. He couldn't leave the place he had known all his life and take up his abode among strangers. He said if she really loved him, she wouldn't ask such a sacrifice of him. She said if he truly loved her, he would willingly make such a sacrifice. And so it was stalemate, and they parted. The young man was heartbroken, and wondered if he had been in the wrong. Before he could change his mind, however, he heard the maid was to be married, to the son of a fairly well-to-do farmer, who could buy her the pretty things she craved, and their wedding day was fixed.

Then his father died, and the young man was left alone in the hut. It was more than he could bear, and he decided to sell up their few sticks, and walk to Coventry to find work. He made all his arrangements, and was anxious to be gone. The thought of seeing his love become the wife of another was intolerable to him.

It was his last night in the hut. His tools and few belongings were packed into one small bag, and on the morrow when the first streaks of daylight appeared in the sky, he would set forth. He sat by the remains of the fire, and his thoughts were sorrowful ones.

Outside it was an icy night, with a snow storm raging. The water in the canal was frozen, and the wind howled about the crooked chimney. He realised he would have difficulties walking to Coventry, but he would have to manage it. Suddenly there came a knock upon his door. He couldn't think who could be visiting him on such a night, and he was reluctant to open up. The knocking continued, more urgent, and when he at last got to his feet, and lifted the latch, the girl stood upon his threshold.

She was soaked to the skin, and her white gown was torn and ragged. Her face was whiter than the snow that clung to her hair, and her eyes were swollen with weeping.

She rushed into the hut and crouched above the fire, shaking with cold and racked with sobs.

'What have you come here for?' cried the young man. 'Today is your wedding day. What has happened?'

Wildly weeping, the girl told her story. It was an old and familiar one. She had been dressing for her wedding, she said. The torn and ragged gown that now clung about her was of white silk, her bridal gown. As she was about to set out for the church, there came a boy with a note from her lover. He had gone; run off to Australia with his brother, leaving the maid jilted, virtually on the steps of the altar. 'So I've come back to you' she said at length. 'I know now I was wrong, and I've been punished, so I've come back.'

The young man would have been less than human had he not felt a slight twinge of righteous satisfaction, but he said 'Too late my maid. It's too late. I've sold up here, and tomorrow I leave. There is no future for us. It is too late.'

'You forsake me too!' the girl wailed, and gathering her rags about her, she thrust him aside and ran from the hut into the icy storm. Pausing only to pick up a lantern, the young man followed her, but she had disappeared into the snowy night. He could see nothing, although he searched long and hard. He was fearful that the girl may have missed her footing and slid silently into the waters of the canal. He looked carefully along the canal banks, and was relieved to find the ice there unbroken.

He did not know which way the girl had gone, for the steadily falling snow had obliterated her footprints, just as it was now filling his own. He returned to the hut and prayed the girl had made her way safe home to her mother's hovel on Yarningale Common.

On the following morning he set off on the long and arduous walk to the great city of Coventry, where he worked with a cabinet maker. His heart was full of regrets for what might have been, but he resolutely turned his face away from the past. For some years he worked in Coventry, and then he moved further afield, always readily finding work, for there was great skill in his hands. After some ten years, a wave of homesickness came upon him, and he resolved to return to his native heath. He had never forgotten the girl, nor had he heard a word of her since that dreadful night. He assumed that she would by now be married, and perhaps the mother of a growing family. But he had been away from home too long, and he had a yearning to be in familiar places.

One winter's day, he set off on his long walk home. It was dark when he reached the outskirts of the village he had once known. Snow was falling, the paths were icy, and a thick freezing mist made it impossible to see ahead. He stumbled many times, and his face was scratched where he blundered into unfriendly bushes. He headed for the canal and the woodman's hut where he had spent his childhood, but after ten years in the big cities, his countryman's sense of direction was blunted, and he found to his horror that he was lost.

He paused, his breath was coming in gasps; he was exhausted, and didn't know which way to turn. Quite suddenly, in front of him he saw a glimmer of white, a shapeless shape, and seemed compelled to walk towards it. As he neared the shape, he saw he was on the banks of the canal, now again covered with ice. He should have felt frightened, but somehow the shape, which glimmered and undulated towards him, comforted him. A voice said 'Follow me and you'll be safe' and icy fingers caught hold of his hand. He found himself being lead forward, and he had no choice but to follow.

The pressure of the icy fingers upon his own was gentle, and he knew he was no longer lost amid these freezing wastes. He stumbled along, his boots slipping on the icy ground, and there in front of him was the old hut, ramshackle now and tumbledown, but still his old home. 'You are safe now . . .' said the soft voice, and he recognised it as the voice of his long lost love. 'You are safe now . . .' and the icy fingers let go of his hand.

The shimmer of light gathered itself about a tree, and then faded, slowly, slowly. He heard the sound of soft breathing, and a sob. He walked towards the tree, drawn by the sight of something hung upon it. It was a scrap of white silk; the white silk she had been wearing; the torn and tattered bridal gown in which she had come to him on that last night.

He stood still, the scrap of silk in his hand. Then he heard the splash, right up beneath the lock gates, where the water constantly runs and never freezes no matter how hard the ice further down the banks. And then he knew what had happened on that dreadful night ten years ago. He knew his maid was a maid still, and he would never see her again in this life.

He put the scrap of silk next to his heart, and kept it there to the end of his days.

6

Home Is Where The Heart Is?

THE pretty bustling village of Wootton Wawen sits astride the main route between Stratford-upon-Avon and Birmingham, and is dominated by the superb 17th century Palladian mansion of Wootton Hall, standing amid parkland on the banks of the river Alne.

Wootton Wawen is one of the earliest settlements in Warwickshire, and with such a long history of human habitation spanning the centuries, it is no wonder that ghosts abound at Wootton Hall, although none of them seem to have given rise to much disquiet.

On a pediment above the door are the arms of the Smith family, 'Regi semper fidelis' (Always faithful to the King) and indeed they were. Sir Charles Smith stood alongside King Charles I in the English Civil War and in 1643 was created 1st Viscount Carington for his loyal service.

After the hostilities, after the King was so horribly beheaded and Oliver Cromwell held the reins of Government, Lord Carington was forced to flee to France like so many other faithful Royalists. In 1665 he was murdered by his valet at Pontoise. No details are known of this crime other than that the motive was robbery, and after killing his master, the valet fled. He was caught and put to death.

Lord Carington's friends buried his body at Pontoise, but his heart they put into an oak box and brought back to England, to Wootton Hall, his home. This may sound a trifle macabre, but it was not at all unusual in those days for a body to be buried in one place, whilst the heart was removed for burial to the place most loved by the deceased person. There are several 'heart burials' in small Midlands churches. However, Lord Carington's heart did not get properly buried. No one knew what had become of it, except that it was at Wootton Hall – somewhere. Lord Carington could not rest in peace.

It was in the 19th century that the disturbances were first reported, although it is extremely likely that they had been going on for a long time before this. The hall was let, and tenants talked of doors opening and closing of their own volition; or refusing to open at all. Of things that bumped and clashed in the night. It seems that dogs bristled and refused to enter rooms, and there was an occasional inexplicable atmosphere of chill. But although such things were a bit of a nuisance, they did not apparently frighten anybody very much, or cause any real upset.

It was not until 1937 that the mystery was solved. Captain Hubert Berkeley had lived at the hall, and he wrote:

> 'The Carington heart was found in a heart shaped oak box lined with velvet. Wm Keyte (the bailiff on the estate) found it in a cupboard and didn't know what to do with it. He put it in a grave when he was burying someone in the Catholic cemetery . . .'

Which someone, and which grave in the Catholic cemetery, quite close to the hall, no one knows, but it may now be assumed perhaps that Lord Carington lies quiet.

According to report, Mr Keyte found the heart box when he was turning out some ancient cupboards in a small attic in the roof where nobody ever went, and it must have given him something of a shock. It seems inconceivable that in more than 250 years no one had discovered it before.

Wootton Hall was also the childhood home of Maria Anne Smythe, later to become Mrs Fitzherbert, the morganatic wife of the Prince Regent, who married her secretly in 1785. Mrs Fitzherbert returned often to the hall and it was here the Prince visited her. Close by is an ancient milestone telling us it is 100 miles to London. The Prince was wont to say with a sigh that he wished he were 'an hundred miles from London' and his closest cronies realised he was referring to Wootton Hall and his devoted Maria.

Poor Mrs Fitzherbert did not have a very happy time. She was a widow, and a Catholic when the marriage took place, and as soon as it became known, it was declared invalid under the Royal Marriage Act. That must have been bad enough, but later the Prince Regent declared it had never taken place at all! Yet he maintained his 'liaison' with Maria until 1803.

The Prince of Wales feathers in the 'Boudoir' bedroom are a reminder of this, and it is in this room that the grey lady, supposedly the wraith of the unhappy Maria, has been seen. She also makes her presence felt in other parts of the house where, although she is not seen, the air is suddenly filled with the scent of a delicate perfume. She is a very gentle ghost and bothers no one. It is believed that since some of the happiest times in Maria Fitzherbert's life were those spent at the Hall, this is where she returned, and where she wishes to remain.

A Wootton Hall ghost that did cause a bit of a problem, though, was wont to appear in the dairy, built on to the other side of the house. Nervous dairymaids would have to be either soothed or spoken sharply to when they came rushing out of the dairy with the tale of a tall man sitting in a chair in the corner. Apparently he did not seem to menace them, or show any ill-will towards them. But there he was, looking at them.

One may imagine with what exasperation busy housekeepers would tell a succession of nervous village girls to get on with their work and stop being silly! But as it transpired, perhaps they weren't being so silly after all.

In 1861 the old dairy was pulled down, having outlasted its usefulness, and beneath the flagstones in the corner where dairymaids had so often seen the tall man in his chair, two skeletons were found. They were those of a man and a woman, and the male skeleton was that of an exceptionally tall man.

They had been buried beneath the well-worn flagstones for

a long time, and it was quite impossible to establish their identity. But there existed in the Smith family a legend that once upon a time one of the sons of the house had run off with and secretly married a dairymaid. With the passage of the years, the details had been forgotten, but it is possible that they had never been allowed to run off at all, and thus bring disgrace to the family. There is a distinct possibility that they had got no further than their rendezvous in the old dairy, and had there been summarily despatched. Poor conjecture, but not perhaps unreasonable.

7

Ghosts of the Road

THROUGHOUT the centuries Warwickshire roads have always been much travelled since it is in the very centre of England, and anyone moving north to south, east to west, or vice versa must needs pass through it at some point. With so many travellers, it is therefore little wonder that many highwaymen had their 'beat' in a county where handsome pickings were to be had.

Wild open spaces like Dunsmore Heath or Wolvey Heath were frankly dangerous and few travellers escaped with their purse intact. Gangs of thieves, lone robbers and cutpurses roamed the countryside a couple of hundred years ago, and they all had their retreats, inns or 'safe' houses where they could hide out, pay up and no questions asked. Highwaymen made a good living off the main routes and many of them are said to still haunt the stretches of road that proved so lucrative to them in their lifetime.

It must have been a frightening experience to find yourself on a deserted stretch of road, urging on a tired horse, darkness closing in around you, and up ahead a group of trees where in all probability a masked robber lay in wait.

The most famous highwayman of them all, Dick Turpin, found a stretch of the old Roman road, Watling Street, running between Nuneaton and the border of Leicestershire, a source of good profit. This was a part of the main route between London and Holyhead, along which were many coaches full of passengers with fat purses.

Turpin was born in Essex in 1705 and when still quite young took to the roads as his career. He was clever enough to realise that the best way to avoid capture was to move around and not to overdo any particular stretch. When working his Warwickshire beat he is said to have made an inn at Dunchurch his hideout, but whether this was the Dun Cow or the Lion is not absolutely clear. He formed a tenuous partnership with the notorious Birmingham highwayman, Tom King. Birmingham was, of course, in those days, in Warwickshire anyway.

Turpin was hanged at York on 10th April 1739, and Tom King was burned to death in Sutton Park, Birmingham. King is still said to haunt the site of his death.

Dick Turpin still rides his particular stretch of Watling Street and has been sighted many times. He is described as wearing a tricorne hat and a red coat, and riding a black mare. The sight of him once caused a group of intrepid motor cyclists to swerve to avoid what they saw as a mounted figure moving rapidly towards them. Then, as suddenly as it appeared, it disappeared – into the hedge, and was gone!

There was a theory that Turpin concealed some of his ill-gotten gains in the deserted village of Stretton Baskerville, not far from his beat. This lost village, one of many in the county, once had a thriving population and a church, but in the days of the wool trade, the landowner turned the tenants out and enclosed the fields to rear sheep. Stretton Baskerville was in ruins by the mid 15th century, as recorded by John Rous, the Warwickshire historian, and it became the haunt of those on the other side of the law, including the redoubtable Dick, who is supposed to have buried his gold beneath the church. Although many people have searched these ruins, no long lost hoard of gold has ever come to light as far as we know.

At Priors Marston, where Warwickshire moves towards the Northamptonshire border, there was an inn called The Roebuck, more commonly referred to as Rogues' Hall. It was the hideout of bands of robbers who preyed upon the drovers using the old Welsh Road. Herds of cattle were moved along this road, through Brownhills, Kenilworth and Southam, and on to markets in London. Drovers used it to avoid paying tolls, and returned from London the same way, with their pockets stuffed with money. Out came the pack from Rogues' Hall, to attack and rob. Sounds of violence and altercation are still reputed to be heard around here.

Another quite famous highwayman, who rejoiced in the name of Bendigo Mitchell, used the Old Inn (now a private house) at Bishops Tachbrook as his headquarters. He worked alone, and his particular beat was the Fosse Way around Moreton Morrell, but he was caught and subsequently hanged in Warwick in 1772, leaving his ghost to still ride his stretch.

At Fenny Compton there exists the story of a local highwayman who was something of a Robin Hood character in that he robbed the rich to give to the poor, which was quite clever of him really. In this way, the 'poor' who were being 'given to' would keep their mouths shut! This romantic gentleman of the road operated around Fenny Compton in the 16th century, and was so adept at evading capture it was said of him that his horse had an enchanted bridle, magnanimously donated by the fairies, impressed with his goodness of heart.

Be that as it may, the man eventually got his come-uppance, and was carted off to Warwick, where he was sentenced to be hanged. However, his luck still held, if you like to look at it in a roundabout way, for he managed to take his own life before anyone else could do it for him, thus avoiding the ignominy of the public scaffold. He is believed to have buried his not inconsiderable loot in a field at Fenny Compton, known as the 'hen and chickens' where it is said he still lingers watching over it. The 'hen and chickens' came in for a lot of attention in the years that followed, but no one found anything. At least, no one ever owned up to finding anything. If they did unearth a few gold coins, they probably kept very quiet about it!

The Gaydon Inn on the main route from Warwick to Banbury, and just outside the village of Gaydon, was the haunt of John Smith Snr, the leader of a formidable gang who terrorised the neighbourhood hereabouts. He was caught and hanged, but only two years later, his son, John Smith Jnr, who worked the same beat as his late father, was arrested quite close to the inn. He had a very long list of hold-ups and robberies to answer for, and they were taking no chances with him. Rather than cart him off to Warwick at night when, for all 'they' knew, his accomplices could spring out at them and effect his escape, they locked him up in the attic of the Gaydon Inn until morning. He whiled away the midnight hour carving his initials upon a beam, and his ghost is said to walk the attic still.

Unlike many of his ilk John Smith Jnr was not hung in chains near the scene of his crime, after his hanging in 1789, as was usually the case. His sweetheart, Elizabeth Beere, who must have had the patience of a saint, wept and pleaded for his dead body, and was given leave to take it away for burial. The thoughtful girl had brought with her a donkey for just this purpose, and trudged all the way back home from Warwick, with the dead John Smith Jnr roped across the back of the animal. What comment the sight of this extraordinary trio moving along the main route between Warwick and Banbury brought forth is not, alas, on record.

The main route between Stratford-upon-Avon and Oxford (now the A34) was also frequented by highwaymen, two of whom attacked and robbed a farmer near the spot known as Clifford Chambers turn. The man was returning home from market in Stratford-upon-Avon, and had money on him. The two men lay in wait, and as the lone traveller approached, they sprang upon him, attacking him with such violence that they killed him. They then stole his money, and flung his body into a pit not far from the roadside. The pit is no longer there, but the poor farmer is said to appear from time to time, wringing his hands, and pleading for mercy. The highwaymen apparently got away with it that time.

8

One Handed Boughton

IT is not often that a ghost moves with its family from one house to another, since they usually seem to remain in surroundings familiar to them. One Handed Boughton was an exception, and it was not until after the end of the Second World War that he was finally laid to rest after a rampage that spanned several centuries.

The origin of One Handed Boughton is somewhat obscure. Some believe him to have lived around the time of Elizabeth I, a period which has proved very popular for the origination of ghostly legends. Others believe he dates from much earlier. Some stories indicate that he lost his hand in an accident, although they do not specify what kind of an accident. Other more colourful tales take the view that his hand was cut off because he moved the boundary markers between his land and that of his neighbour, to his own advantage.

Whatever the truth, this rumbustious squire was a Boughton, one of the long established family of Boughtons at Lawford Hall, Little Lawford, near Rugby. Here One Handed Boughton rip-roared about the neighbourhood in his lifetime, terrorising maidservants, chasing nubile local females, carousing wildly, and taking unto himself any odd bits of land that he thought he could get away with, if the stories told of him are only even half true.

Death did not subdue him apparently, for despite being properly buried, he refused to lie down, and his noisy ghost, fleshless yet fleshy, red-faced and roaring, was still very much in occupation at Lawford Hall.

A very persistent and troublesome ghost was One Handed Boughton, and his activities were by no means confined, for he wandered quite far afield, always returning to Lawford Hall. Clad in a red velvet coat, his appearance heralded by shouting and the crack of a whip, he careered through the village in a tumbledown coach, leaping gates, driving like the wind, and terrifying all who were abroad at the time. Inside the house, the room which had been his bedchamber, and where it is assumed death finally overcame him, was the scene of nightly activity. Chairs were overturned, tables moved, things flung upon the floor, as his heavy footsteps pounded back and forth.

It became impossible to persuade servants to remain in the house, and few people, if any at all, would dare venture out after dark anywhere in the neighbourhood.

That rather august body, the Warwickshire Naturalists and Archaeologists Field Club heard of One Handed Boughton in 1886, when one of its members, historian Mr M H Bloxham, told them of a very old man, almost 100 years of age, whom he had known when he was himself a youth. The old man, John Wolf by name, had been born close to Lawford Hall, where his mother worked as a cleaner. The boy often went to the hall, and waited to walk home with her. He distinctly recalled the housekeeper saying to his mother 'Make haste Esther, get your supper and be off home, for One Handed Boughton will be here soon, and you would not like to meet him!' According to old John Wolf, many locals encountered this colourful character, despite their best efforts to keep out of his way.

Early in the 18th century, Lawford Hall came into the ownership of Sir Edward Boughton, who held the title from 1722, and life became a little more gracious and more sociable. However, the activities of One Handed Boughton still continued in and around his old home, and this caused Sir Edward considerable embarrassment. Guests invited to sup with the Baronet hurriedly excused themselves and left the dining table; those invited to remain overnight departed in haste without a backward glance as soon as daylight dawned. Sir Edward's attempts at hospitality were constantly defeated by his troublesome ancestor.

Sir Edward felt the time had come to do something about it, to lay the ghost once and for all. He was finding the situation intolerable.

After searching about for a solution, it was decided that the ghost of One Handed Boughton must be exorcised. Accordingly twelve clergymen, brave and hardy souls, assembled one night in the bedchamber, the heart of the spectral activities. The door was locked behind them, and each of the twelve lit the candle he held in his hand. The process of the exorcism began and, one by one, the candles flickered and died, extinguished by a non-existent breeze or the ghostly breath of One Handed Boughton. Only one candle flame remained: that held by Parson Hall of nearby Great Hanborough, the leader of the party. He it was who succeeded in capturing the recalcitrant spirit in a bottle which he then proceeded to cork up securely. One Handed Boughton was captured. But to accomplish this, Parson Hall had to strike a bargain with him. The bothersome and noisy ghost could have two hours freedom every night, from midnight, when he could wander at will about the estate he once owned, provided he went quietly back into the bottle when his time was up so that the family and the locals had some respite from his rip-roaring antics.

The bottle was then sealed up with wax and the twelve clergymen went in solemn procession to a pool in the grounds of the hall. With due ceremony they flung the bottle into the middle of the deep pool, where it promptly sank from view.

After this, One Handed Boughton kept to his part of the bargain. He wandered for only two hours each night, but during these two hours he still made his presence felt. His bedchamber was kept permanently locked, for none of the servants could be persuaded to enter and clean it. He roared about the estate in his old coach, red velvet coat flapping, and most locals still kept within doors after dark. After the exorcism, however, although One Handed Boughton might still be a nuisance, the fear of him had somewhat abated.

Sir Edward was not entirely rid of his troublesome forbear,

but he strove to keep to his part of the bargain as well. One day whilst walking on his estate with a friend, Sir Francis Skipwith, this gentleman looked into the pool wherein old One Handed reposed safe in his bottle. Sir Francis remarked that the pool looked positively alive with fish, and he rather fancied a spot of fishing. Sir Edward politely replied that this would be quite impossible, since the pool contained the ghost of his ancestor, and he would not have him disturbed.

Sir Edward Boughton died in 1772, and in 1780 tragedy struck the family at Lawford Hall. Sir Theodosius, the young baronet, and son of Sir Edward, was murdered; poisoned, it is alleged, by laurel water. His brother-in-law, Captain John Donnellan, was charged with the crime. He stood trial at Warwick, was found guilty and hanged, a sentence felt by many to be a miscarriage of justice. This set the seal of doom upon Lawford Hall. Sir Edward's widow and her daughter, the sister of the murdered baronet, and wife, now widow, of Donnellan, were all that was left of the family, and they did not wish to continue living at Lawford Hall.

In 1790, the old place was razed to the ground as a place 'accursed'. Workmen engaged on the demolition had to be paid extra money, for such was the evil legend hovering around the hall, nobody would undertake the job.

The widow of Captain Donnellan married again, and the family became the Boughton-Leighs of Brownsover Hall, near Rugby, not too far off from the old Boughton home, Lawford Hall.

This move must have greatly upset the spirit of One Handed Boughton, for locals reported that he no longer confined his appearances to his old home, but had taken to driving his tumbledown coach around Brownsover Hall, and making just as much of a nuisance of himself as ever. Obviously he decided he belonged to the family rather than to the place!

Some 25 years or so after Lawford Hall was demolished, a youngster fishing in the pool there, dredged up the sealed bottle containing the spirit of One Handed Boughton. According to the reports of the Warwickshire Naturalists and Archaeologists Field Club, this bottle was described as seeming to contain a 'ghostly substance' and it was put on exhibition in Rugby. What old One Handed must have thought of this is not on record, but as an obvious extrovert, he probably enjoyed it.

The bottle was eventually returned to the Boughton-Leigh family, and was kept securely locked in a cupboard in a locked room at Brownsover Hall. The spectre continued to enjoy his two hours freedom every night, but now the family had got quite used to him, and took little notice of his bumping around.

During the Second World War, Brownsover Hall, like many such large houses, was taken over for important research work, although the family continued to live in a part of it. The newcomers, all from far afield, knew nothing of the legend of One Handed Boughton, and yet reported many strange happenings, eerie feelings, and the sound of things going bump in the night. Nightwatchmen patrolling the premises were startled at the sound of overturning chairs and footsteps emanating from a room which they knew to be empty and securely locked. They often told of the sense of someone or something brushing past them along passages. Dogs would bristle and refuse to move. More than once, the sound of wheels on the drive had caused someone to open the door thinking a visitor had arrived, only to find no sign of any vehicle and the drive totally deserted.

Once or twice people saw the door of the locked room, wherein the important bottle reposed in its cupboard, open and close of its own volition.

After the war, the strangers based at Brownsover Hall left to return to their own homes, and the Boughton-Leigh family decided to leave too. Brownsover Hall was sold and turned into a hotel.

But what to do with One Handed Boughton? The problem was solved, and solved forever. The bottle was handed to the agent who looked after the Boughton-Leigh family affairs, and he, accompanied by one member of the family, buried the bottle deep in solid concrete, in a secret place which has never been revealed. This must have laid the ghost of One Handed Boughton for all time, for he has never been seen again, nor has there been any sign of his unwelcome presence anywhere.

Perhaps not even the most determined spirit can emerge from beneath several feet of concrete.

9

The Battle in the Skies

EDGEHILL is reputed to be the most haunted battlefield in England, and a recital of the extraordinary phenomena witnessed here from time to time would fill an entire book on its own! For many years, on Edgehill Night, 23rd October, ghost hunters, serious and sceptical alike, have taken up positions on the hillside overlooking the plain, hoping that the strange manifestations would once again appear before them, but without success. Perhaps they should have remembered that the calendar has changed since 1642 and twelve days were 'lost'.

Edgehill was the first battle of the English Civil War; the first time King Charles I, and the Parliament, with their opposing forces, met face to face. The battle began with a single musket shot fired in anger early on the morning of that bitterly cold 23rd October, and raged throughout the day. Many were the valiant deeds and acts of great courage and bravery carried out by men on both sides, and the fighting was as bitter as the wind that blew across that flat land. As night began to close in, both sides fell back, leaving the field littered with dead and wounded. Reports of the number of dead vary enormously from between 1,500 and 6,000, and it is believed that many wounded were saved by the extreme cold of the night which lowered their body temperature and stopped them from bleeding to death.

The battle was by no means conclusive; neither side 'won'. The Roundheads fell back to the village of Kineton, where they found shelter and 'borrowed' or stole food and fodder. The King's forces moved off towards the town of Banbury.

The local inhabitants, simple peasants for the most part, had gazed in wonder at the sight of armed men, cannon and ordinance, and had probably heaved a great sigh of relief when they all moved off. The whole event which had, for a few days, disrupted their particular bit of countryside could now be pushed to the back of their minds as they got on with the chores of their simple living, when suddenly they were once again plunged into the depths of fear.

One Saturday night, just before Christmas of that year, three shepherds walked together from their homes in Kineton to check on their flocks grazing near the site of the battle. They are described as 'poor ignorant men' who probably had no thought in their heads at this time other than the welfare of their sheep and how quickly they could get back home in the warm.

As they approached Edgehill field, they were halted by the sound of a great noise, and a light in the sky so bright it dazzled them. They were terrified, and amid the torn and crumpled turf where Englishmen had so lately fought and killed each other, they stood rooted to the spot, gazing upwards. Within the circle of the great light, in the darkened skies above them, they watched the battle being re-enacted. They could not tear their gaze from it, and so real was it that they saw faces, heard the thunder of horse's hoofs, the cries of command. They shuddered to the roar of the cannon, and about their heads they felt the whistle of air from flying musket balls. With increasing horror, they listened to the screams of the dying and the groans of the wounded; the distant sound of the cornet and muffled drum beat, and the harsh sound of steel meeting steel from clashing sabres.

This continued unabated for three hours, during which time the three shepherds were completely unable to move, and all the time, in their fear, they thought their last hour on earth had come upon them.

The great light eventually died from the skies and the images faded. Only then were they able to force their legs to move, and to run as fast as they could back into Kineton to tell their story. Despite the lateness of the hour, they knocked upon the door of the Minister, Mr Samuel Marshall, and a local Justice, Mr William Wood. These two august gentlemen heard the shepherds' tale with some scepticism, but on the following night, accompanied by a few other local notables, they went themselves to the battlefield. The same ghostly re-enactment occurred all over again, exactly as the shepherds had described it, and the entire party fled homewards.

For several nights the spectral tumult was witnessed by many people, and the whole area was in a state of abject terror. We are told people hid themselves; others lay 'sweating halfe smothered in their beds . . .' Many women miscarried, and stout hearted men confessed their fear of death. So great was this fear that Samuel Marshall and William Wood set off for Oxford to seek audience with the King and apprise him of the strange circumstances.

The King, upon hearing the sorry tale, immediately sent Colonel Lewis Kirke and Captains Dudley and Wainman, together with three others, to see just what was afoot. They were not disappointed, for they too witnessed the ghostly battle in the skies. They, who had seen the reality on the 23rd October, saw it all again, exactly as it had happened. They heard the sounds and cries, and they saw the faces of their dead comrades. They returned immediately and reported the truth of the story to the King.

It had been suggested that these manifestations might have been caused by some of the dead remaining on the field unburied, hidden from view amid furze and vegetation. Accordingly a search was made, and true enough, some bodies were found. These were given a proper and reverent Christian burial, and everyone hoped this would put an end to the terror engulfing them. But it was not to be. The great light, and the ghost battle continued for some time until it eventually faded out.

Shortly afterwards, a pamphlet entitled 'The New Yeare's Wonder' was issued by a London printer, Mr Thomas Jackson, who gave a colourful and exact description of the occurrences. It sold well!

Among those who lost their lives at Edgehill was Royalist Henry Kingsmill, from Hampshire. He too left a legend to linger after him. He rode into the battle on a great white horse, and it is this loyal creature which still remains, wandering riderless and unchecked, looking for its late master. The sound of ghostly hoofs may be heard on the 23rd October, when its great white misty shape looms out of the darkness, before it turns again on its eternal search.

Kingsmill was buried at nearby Radway, and some time after the end of the hostilities, his mother, Lady Bridget Kingsmill, caused an effigy to be erected to the memory of her brave son. Time and weather have not dealt kindly with this stone figure, but after 350 years it still remains. Legend has it that upon the anniversary of the battle, a small posy of flowers is found upon it. Who so honours the memory of Henry Kingsmill is not known.

Also legendary is the tale of the bloodstained barn, now long gone, where a wounded Royalist is supposed to have taken refuge. The blood that stained its wooden walls ran afresh every 23rd October.

Local land names bear witness to this past event. Grave-ground Coppice is where many of the dead were hurriedly interred in a mass grave, and where it is said local dogs and horses refuse to venture. Red Road, a mere bridle track now, is supposed to have once run red with the blood of the wounded, escaping from the conflict. On the 23rd October, in the dead of the night, legend has it you can still hear the shuffle of their booted feet as they limpingly make their way to safety.

There are quite a lot of ghosts left over from the battle of Edgehill, quite apart from the manifestations on the actual battlefield. At Lighthorne and at Leek Wootton there are wraiths of young women weeping and wailing, thought to be the wives, now widows, of soldiers who died.

Middleton Hall, on the Northamptonshire side of the county, has the ghost of an Edgehill messenger. Legend has it that the man rode frantically, whipping his horse into a great lather, to bring news of the battle to the Willoughby family at the hall. Crossing the drawbridge, the weary horse slipped, and both man and horse drowned in the deep moat below. When the moat was filled in, in 1869, bones were found which lend credulity to this story.

At Warmington it is recorded that many of those wounded at Edgehill sought sanctuary there, mostly to die of their injuries. The vicar recorded the burial of one, Alexander Gourdin, who has a small headstone to mark his last resting place; he also recorded having buried seven more whose names he did not know, and that many others were buried 'in the fields and wynds of Warmington' where they fell. They do say that sometimes at night, you can still hear cries of pain from those who came to Warmington to die.

It is no longer possible to venture anywhere near the site of this famous battle. The entire area was taken over by army authorities some years ago, and there is now tight security. But thereby hangs another tale.

10

The Ghost Coach of Ufton

SOUTHAM, not far from the Northamptonshire border, is a pleasant little town, with some lovely old buildings, including a pub called 'The Mint' where centuries ago Southam tokens were produced. The town's prosperity has waxed and waned, and the building of turnpike roads in the 18th century brought commercial success. Southam was conveniently sited where two important routes crossed. The north-south route is now the Coventry to Banbury road, and the east-west route was the Welsh Drovers Road, much used to take cattle to the London markets. It is now called simply the Welsh Road.

The new turnpikes brought the coaching trade well to the fore in Southam, and the Craven Arms became the foremost of the town's coaching inns. Eighty horses were kept here at all times, and so brisk was the trade that the landlord had to build six small cottages close by to house additional ostlers. The Craven Arms was burned to the ground in 1742, but rapidly rose from the ashes, and flourished again.

From here the 'Royal Mail' left for London every night at 8.20 pm and every morning at 6.30 am for Birmingham. The 'Crown Prince' did the run for Birmingham via Warwick every afternoon, and the 'Regulator' went three times a week to London. In addition there was the 'Tally Ho', the 'Sovereign', the 'Eagle' and the 'Nimrod' plying their way to Lutterworth, Leicester, Rugby and Oxford.

It seems coach travel was inexpensive and convenient, and it was possible to travel the length and breadth of the country quite easily, if a little uncomfortably.

Although little trace remains of this flourishing period, with a little imagination one can visualise the excitement created by the sound of the post horn, the many wheels clattering over the cobbles, and the ostlers running in all directions to change the horses and get the coach on its way on time.

The drivers of these great coaches were proud of their skill, and of their smart turn-out, and doubtless boasted a little to each other as they waited for a change of horses and refreshment. Wagers on record times were quite usual, and it was one such wager that lead to a tragedy.

The road leading north from Southam towards Leamington Spa goes through the tiny village of Ufton, about two miles out of the town. Ufton has a long steep hill, with a sharp bend at the top, where its church stands upon a lofty rocky outcrop. This required considerable expertise to negotiate, particularly in bad weather.

The story goes that one young, and perhaps boastful, driver accepted a wager from his cronies at the inn that he would make Leamington Spa and back in record time. The landlord of the inn kept the wager, and off went the young driver, with a coachload of passengers, and six mettlesome fresh horses.

Once out of the town he whipped the horses up to breakneck speed as they approached Ufton. But alas his skill was not as great as he thought! It was raining heavily, and there was a lot of mud. The coach failed to successfully negotiate the sharp bend, and slipping and sliding, the horses could not regain their foothold. Down the hill careered the runaway coach, which overturned several times, landing in a broken heap at the bottom. The driver and all the passengers had to be rescued, and all were severely injured. Two of the horses were so badly hurt that they had to be shot then and there, while the others had to be cut from their traces.

Now, they tell me, on wild and stormy nights this coach may still be seen, being dragged along by frightened wild-eyed lathered horses.

The story of the ghost coach is legend in the area. But honesty compels me to admit I have not been able to find any factual report of the incident, or the name of either the coach or the driver.

I think such incidents are typical of the coaching era in any town, and there can be little doubt that it did in fact happen. The road through Ufton is now wide and open, but the hill and the sharp bend still remain, so that it takes only a little imagination to visualise how a great lumbering coach and six savagely whipped horses failed to make the descent safely.

11

The Ghosts of Arrow Spring

THE pretty village of Arrow, just outside Alcester, curves around the edge of the parkland surrounding Ragley Hall, a superb Palladian mansion built in the 17th century by the 1st Earl of Conway, whose successor, the 8th Marquess of Hertford still lives here, with his family. There are no ghosts inside the hall, although some 50 years ago, there was 'rustic talk' about the ghost of a 'black man' but this probably stemmed from and became entirely mixed up with the story of Popham Seymour Conway, cousin to the 1st Earl, who was killed in a duel, and whose ancestry could, possibly, be traced right back to a black hermit of the 7th century! Of such stuff are legends made.

However, although the hall might be apparition-free, a spring on the edge of the estate, between Arrow and Dunnington, has a positive plethora of female spirits, whose stories have become so enmeshed it is impossible to disentangle them.

In 1833 an excavation near to this spring revealed the skeleton of an Anglo-Saxon lady of the manor, buried as was the custom, with her jewellery and a small dagger, all of very fine workmanship. Whether the dagger was the cause of her death is not known. But here her shadowy figure has been seen, bending down to drink deeply at the spring.

Another 'white lady' is also said to haunt this spot, and the area immediately surrounding it, although this time the description varies. This one is said to be young, dark haired, beautiful, clad in white silk. The legend has grown up that she was a lady's maid to Maria Fagniani, the wife of the 3rd

Marquess of Hertford (1777-1842) who came with her mistress to Ragley Hall. Here, she developed an attachment to a manservant, noted for his extremely jealous disposition. Their attachment was no secret, and neither were their quarrels. One morning they were found to have gone, both disappeared during the night, and they were never heard of again. There was much gossip and speculation. Some thought they had run off and eloped; others decided among themselves there had been another, much worse quarrel and the girl had been killed by her lover, who must have hidden her body somewhere in the vicinity, and then run off to escape justice. The lady's maid, if indeed it is she, lingers in the park, wandering towards the spring, her silk gown brushing the grass but making no noise. However, there is no record of any murdered body ever being found anywhere near here, so if this was indeed the fate of the lovely young Italian girl, we shall never know.

Another story of the spring concerns the ghost of an old and sprightly lady, clad in bonnet and shawl, who frequently appeared in front of coach travellers, begging for a ride. She appeared grateful when helped into the coach, but when it stopped to allow her to alight, it was invariably found to be empty. The little old lady had dissolved into thin air. Legend has it that the bones of a little old lady were found near the spring in the last century, and were respectfully buried in the churchyard at Arrow, since which time travellers have been able to go on their way unhindered, as she has never appeared again.

That the Saxon lady was discovered in 1833 is on record, but it does seem rather likely that all three ladies are one and the same, with their stories being distorted and embroidered with each re-telling.

The land on the other side of the road at Arrow is haunted by an unseen creature of the night. This land once belonged to the Burdett family, and in 1477 Thomas Burdett was particularly proud of a large white buck that roamed his domain. However, King Edward IV took it into his head to hunt upon Burdett land in the absence of Thomas, and it was the Royal hand that killed the white buck. Thomas, upon learning of this, made a very heated and indiscreet comment to the effect that he had rather the white buck had sunk his horns into the King's belly first! His enemies, and there are always enemies, reported this indiscretion to the King, who promptly had Thomas beheaded for treason. The unseen creature, whose nocturnal meanderings have been heard, is thought to be the ghost of this white buck, ambling serenely around what used to be its habitat, and beyond which it never ventures.

No one has seen it, but many people are said to have heard it. The countryside is full of strange noises at night, and who is to say which of them stems from the natural and which from the supernatural?

12

The Ghost Blaze at Bagington

BAGINGTON lies on flat land some few miles from the city of Coventry, and the urban sprawl of that great city has now almost encompassed it.

The name 'Bagington' means 'village on a plateau' and here Stone Age men fought each other, leaving weapons to be unearthed many centuries later. Here too, in an open field, was discovered a Roman encampment known as 'The Lunt' and it is thought that Boadicea, the great Queen of the Iceni, engaged her Roman enemies in battle here. From such excavations, as always, unsubstantiated legends have arisen.

West of the church is the site of Bagington Castle, home of the Bagot family since 1381. Here lived Sir William Bagot, loyal friend and trusted minister of Richard II. The King came here in September 1398, with 10,000 men, who camped along the banks of the river Sowe. From Bagington Castle one fine September morning in that year of 1398, Henry Bolingbroke, later King Henry IV, set out for his 'wager of battle' with Thomas Mowbray, Duke of Norfolk, who was staying at Cauldon, just five miles away.

In the year 1400, Sir William Bagot of Bagington was brought to trial, accused of instigating all the 'crimes' of the deposed King. He was flung into the Tower from which he never emerged. In 1403 the Earl of Northumberland was held captive at Bagington after the Battle of Shrewsbury, but sometime after this it began to fall into ruins. John Leland, writing sometime around 1536, describes it as 'now desolatyd. It longidd to the Bargetts . . .' Even Dugdale (*Antiquities of*

Warwickshire) could not discover when it was demolished.

Its remains were excavated by archaeologists in 1935, and they made many interesting finds, including a flight of steps down which Bolingbroke must have trod on that September day in 1398. There were traces of a moat which yielded ancient keys, pottery and gaming counters. The walls of the original castle were believed to be seven ft thick in places.

The site of the old castle is said to be haunted by the headless spectre of a young woman. The archaeologists working there in 1935 were looked upon askance by several rustics who accused them of 'disturbing the ghost'. Sceptical, they enquired 'What ghost?' But indeed the headless lady walks, and apparently walks yet.

No one knows her story, or why she lingers in the place that once housed kings of England. Local legend has it that she was a young and beautiful woman who either lived in the castle of the Bagots, or just stayed there. Maybe she was either a daughter of the house; or she was in some way connected with the extensive retinue that always followed any king. They say she must have been murdered and her body flung into the moat, but the reason for her death and her apparent headless state does not appear in the legend. Perhaps in those lawless days it is not entirely unbelievable that something of the kind might have happened.

She glides, so they say, from the site of the old castle, heading in the direction of the church, and then vanishes. Perhaps she searches for Sir William Bagot, for although he has a brass in the church, dated 1407, according to some historians his body disappeared. He did not emerge from the Tower, and after the year 1400 he was no more. The truth of his end is not known. Whether he was murdered, executed, or just died of great sorrow after his King, Richard II, was murdered at Pontefract, no one has been able to discover.

In the 17th century, the ruined castle came into the hands of the Bromley family, who decided not to attempt the restoration of this now derelict pile, and instead built themselves a fashionable hall close by. This hall was destroyed by fire in 1706. Sir William Bromley, made Speaker of the House of Commons in 1710, rebuilt his house in 1714 with money donated for this purpose by the House of Commons.

But alas, the place seemed fated. On 7th October 1889, it was once again ablaze, and into the flames went all the grand furniture, the collection of pictures and family portraits, a large and notable library of valuable books, and most of the manuscripts and muniments relating to the long history of the Bromleys.

It was a devastating blow, and no rebuilding or restoration was contemplated. For years the shell of the hall stood, a desolate and blackened ruin. Local people became reconciled to the loss of 'the big house', and as weeds and vegetation encroached upon its floors, and entwined its sightless windows, they accepted it would never again rise from the ashes.

Then, one October day some ten years after the fire, a man came running into the village shouting that the hall was on fire. People came dashing out to help; some saw the flames, and a group made their way towards the blazing hall. But when they reached the spot, there were no flames; there was no fire; nor had there been. No smoke lingered, no heat came from the charred walls, and the weeds grew green and verdant.

This happened several times over the years round about the turn of the century. Every time, someone saw flames, and came running to get help, and every time, when people turned out to help, and arrived at the hall, there had been no fire. It caused great wonderment at the time, but has not been witnessed since.

13

The Squire of Chadshunt

A FEW houses scattered along the road that runs between Kineton and Gaydon and a fine and ancient church are all that remains of the once much larger Chadshunt. Like most places in these parts, it has its connection with the battle of Edgehill in a piece of land still called Prince Rupert's Headland. Here the swashbuckling cavalier prince is supposed to have halted his headlong charge through the enemy lines, and re-formed his troop to enter the fray again.

Close to the church stands Chadshunt Hall, once the home of the Newsham family, who came from Yorkshire to Bishops Itchington, where one of them, William, was vicar in 1319. By judicious marriages they acquired land at Chadshunt, and built the hall sometime in the 16th century. By the standards of the time it was not a 'grand mansion' but just a large family home with a considerable acreage. The 18th century squire, Charles Newsham, was much loved and respected. Letters still extant describe him as a most learned man, an excellent scholar, a man of parts and well versed in the law. But alas, he seems to have been the paragon of his line, for it was his grandson who lost the lot!

James Newsham, grandson of Charles, was left fatherless when he was only nine years old. He was, therefore, brought up by his mother, a daughter of James Craggs, the Postmaster General. She had no taste for the quiet rusticity of isolated Warwickshire, and she took the boy from Chadshunt to live the more lively London life she had herself enjoyed. She introduced him at this early age into the doubtful circle of her rich friends, and as he grew older he was caught up in this strata of society. His personal income at that time was £800 a year which had been more than adequate for his father and his grandfather to live comfortably, but it was not apparently adequate for the life he chose to lead. He took heartily to gambling and profligate ways, and although he seemed to love his old home at Chadshunt, this did not stop him from mortgaging it up to the hilt. He borrowed £21,000 on it, and in a very short time, this too was all gone, mostly across the gaming tables.

He died in 1773, leaving no issue, only debts, and the hall was inherited by a distant kinsman, Newsham Peers of Alveston, near Stratford-upon-Avon, who promptly sold it. So after two centuries, there were no Newshams at Chadshunt Hall.

At least, no live Newshams. For according to local legend, the profligate James returns to haunt it. On New Year's Eve, there is the sound of swiftly moving horses, and coach wheels upon the drive, followed by a repeated knocking at the front door. If the door is opened, there is nothing to be seen. No coach, no horses and no Newsham!

It is also on record that 'Squire James' still occasionally rides to hounds, as he used to do when spending time at the hall. In the year 1800 an old shepherd working on the estate told the story of how he had seen the 'old Squire' riding across the fields on his great hunter, followed by some three or four couples of hounds, and how he had taken gates at full gallop, seeming to fly over them. He was described as a large shape with a silvery glow.

Why James should return to haunt the home he foolishly squandered is open to conjecture. It could be put down to remorse, perhaps, since it is entirely on his account that the hall was lost to the Newshams. And after more than 200 years he still hasn't found a way to get it all back.

14

The Elizabethan Ladies of Napton

THE village of Napton-on-the-Hill, east of Southam where Warwickshire approaches Northamptonshire, clings and rambles around the sides of the hill from which it takes its name. From its summit, somewhat windswept and rising 500 or so feet above sea level, it is said that on a clear day you can see seven counties. Although I have stood there many times, I have not yet managed this.

Napton was an important settlement in the Middle Ages, ranking high within the county. It had a relatively large population, and its own weekly market. Its old cottages are built of the local ochre-coloured stone, and once had thatched roofs, but these are gone, replaced by the more modern and conventional roofs.

The ancient church of St Lawrence, high on the hill top, shares with several other Warwickshire villages the legend that it was to have been built elsewhere, on lower ground. But each night, the 'fairies' or 'goblins' came along and removed all the work that the day's labour had accomplished, and carried the stones up to the top of the hill, until the builders got the message, and built it on the hill. It has its origins in the 12th century, and there is an old legend which says that if you take to your heels and run rapidly all around the church three times at midnight, the Devil will appear before you, although why anyone should wish to meet him, I cannot think.

It is the church that is haunted, but the identity of the ghosts has long been the subject of speculation. They are two ladies, always appearing together, and described as being dressed in clothing of the Elizabethan era. Legend has it that these are two sisters who lie buried in the churchyard, but traces of their grave have disappeared, and no one knows who they are. They are to be seen, dressed in their finery and grey woollen cloaks, kneeling deep in prayer in the front pew of the church. They do not apparently materialise very often, and sometimes there is a very long gap between one 'performance' and the next, but according to the story, they have been seen by generations of Napton folk, and at times, people were rather nervous of them.

There is on record the experience of a clergyman in the year 1820. This cleric was filling in for his friend, the regular vicar of Napton, and he took the evening service one Sunday. Not being a local man, he knew nothing of the two Elizabethan ladies, and probably would not have believed it anyway.

After the service, all the congregation had gone, and he was just about to hurry off himself when he realised that he had left his cassock behind in the empty church. He returned to collect it, and as it was getting dark by this time, he carried his lantern. When he walked into the main body of the church, he was disconcerted to see the flame of his lantern turn blue, and cast a rather sinister gloom around him. He could not account for this, but hastened down the aisle when he caught sight of two women kneeling in prayer in the front pew. Thinking that two of his flock had returned to say private prayers, and may perhaps be troubled about something, he moved quietly towards them so as not to disturb their devotions. It was then he realised their clothing was of a bygone period, and quite suddenly, they just disappeared, like the clearing of vapour. As they faded, the flame of his lantern once more reverted to its proper yellow colour. He remained no longer, but grabbed his forgotten cassock and hurried away.

We do not know who these two women are, or were. Indeed we don't know if they are sisters at all, nor why they kneel so wrapped in prayer. It may be perhaps surmised that they are kinswomen of that John Shuckburgh whose name is written up in brass above them. The ladies have not appeared for some years now. Or perhaps it would be more truthful to say they have not been seen, for who knows how many times they might materialise to pray when there is no one about.

There was another ghost at Napton too, this time in the attic of the old vicarage, which is no longer. It seems that in the 19th century, a poor little maidservant who had her room high up in the attic, became pregnant, and ended her earthly troubles by throwing herself from her window. The details of the scandal are lost, but the tale is re-told, and there are those who believe the poor girl returned, her presence being heralded by a feeling of intense cold.

15

The Red Haired Man of Stockton

THE area around Stockton, lying between the towns of Southam and Rugby was once a purely agricultural area, until in the last century the blue Lias beneath the green fields was excavated and the cement industry began. Many cottages were built to house workers in this new industry. Those who once worked the surface of the land now worked beneath it, extracting the necessary ingredient for the cement. Bits of Stockton have thus found their way all over the country and beyond. Many strange prehistoric creatures were found fossilised in the blue Lias and were taken to the Natural History Museum.

It did not last all that long. The cement works are now closed; the canal serves mainly pleasure boats, and the cottages once occupied by cement workers are now lived in by commuters.

Our red haired man, however, pre-dates the cement workings, for he was a farm labourer of the 18th century, working for the farmer whose farmhouse is now, appropriately, called the Blue Lias Inn.

A former landlord of the inn told me the story some years ago, and the nocturnal happenings were recorded even before his time there. There were strange footsteps in the night, pieces of furniture were moved just slightly, doors opened and closed, things went 'bump' and there was an atmosphere of eerie coldness.

This is said to emanate from a scene of great violence enacted in the upper rooms of this building two centuries or more ago. The farmer who worked this land was in a good way of business and employed a considerable amount of local labour. One of these labourers was a young red haired man, who doubtless thought himself a bit of a 'blade' at the time. The farmer was a busy man, and his young wife was probably lonely and bored, so the red haired labourer and the farmer's wife began a clandestine affair. When the farmer was safely out of the way about his business, the young man sneaked into the farmhouse to pursue his amorous adventure. This intrigue probably livened up his otherwise dull life, but it was not to last long.

One day the farmer returned from market earlier than expected, and hearing voices coming from upstairs, went to investigate. There he found his young wife in bed with the red haired labourer. His rage knew no bounds, and dragging the young man to his feet, he savagely attacked and killed him. What happened to the flighty wife, we do not know, but as she does not remain here, it is very likely that she fled for her life!

Since that time, the building has been haunted by the ghost of the farmer, and the ghost of the red haired labourer, although not apparently simultaneously.

Guests staying at the Blue Lias have reported the sound of footsteps in the night, but for some time were at a loss to explain the uneven sound these made. There was always a heavy step, then a lighter one, a sort of 'thump and shuffle'. This was eventually accounted for by the discovery that the farmer had a wooden leg!

The red haired man does not walk though. He merely appears and with such clarity he has at times been mistaken for a customer, and been spoken to, until he disappears, simply melting into the wall. It is thought that the bumps and the moving of furniture re-enact the fight he had with the farmer, the wronged husband, which led to his early death.

16

The Gambler's Ghost

SOME three miles south of Stratford-upon-Avon lies Alscot Park, a most beautiful house, the home of the West family since 1749. Close by, the 'estate villages' of Atherstone-on-Stour, Preston-on-Stour, Wimpstone and Whitchurch ramble round the river Stour.

A 'local' who contributed in large measure to the recording of the history of Warwickshire was the Rev J Harvey Bloom, Rector of Whitchurch at the latter end of the 19th century. An energetic and enthusiastic man, he cycled all over the county collecting endless stories, superstitions and folklore. One of his major tasks, self-imposed, was a survey of all the churchyards in Warwickshire, with details of their headstones and memorials. Many of his unpublished manuscript notes are now in various record offices.

It is the Rev Harvey Bloom who recorded the story of the strange creature said to roam around Alscot Park at night. He says this legend has been handed down in the area for centuries, and describes the beast as 'half man, half calf'. Obviously he was totally sceptical, for he says 'uncanny things do happen at night in the darkness of a deer park. One has the unpleasant sense of being dogged by something one cannot see.' There have been deer in Alscot Park for a very long time. He maintains, however, that when this creature was known to be manifesting itself again, his local parishioners would not stir from their fireside after dark.

His daughter, novelist Ursula Bloom, who wrote much about her childhood and early years in the area, recorded a brush with a much more recent ghost.

As a girl she lived with her parents and her brother in the old rectory at Whitchurch, a somewhat isolated place still, and it would have been much more so in those days. The family were not particularly well-to-do, and having no other means of transport, they used bicycles to visit Stratford-upon-Avon. Indeed, they appear to have vigorously cycled for miles.

Miss Bloom recounts that she and her mother had cycled to Stratford-upon-Avon to visit friends, and were returning home very late. The stable clock at Alscot Park was striking midnight as they passed it. Suddenly, a man appeared, standing at the side of the road leading into the village. So suddenly did this figure appear that Miss Bloom swerved to avoid hitting him. Then just as quickly, he disappeared, only to appear again a few yards ahead.

Ursula Bloom described her feeling of nervousness and cold, but at first thought the man was a local, and wondered why he was here at this time of night. Her mother had not, apparently, seen anything.

The following day, she mentioned this incident to local people, probably seeking to find out who the man was and to tell him to be more careful. To her astonishment, locals told her 'he' was their native ghost.

The story was that in 1882, there was a farmer who enjoyed a fun wager. He accepted a bet that he could ride from his home at Atherstone-on-Stour to the village of Alderminster, at midnight, in the pitch darkness, and arrive in record time.

But alas he didn't arrive at all. His friends awaited him in Alderminster, having laid bets on the event, but they waited in vain.

He was going flat out when a low and overhanging branch of a tree brought him off his mount and he was killed instantly, just as the stable clock at Alscot Park was striking midnight. And this is the time he has been seen, right near the spot where he suffered his fatal fall.

Whether anyone has seen him recently, I do not know. But the lane leading into the village is now wide and metalled, and probably commuters in cars think nothing of the sight of a man merely standing where once grew the tree that caused his death.

17

The Nun's Story

THE village of Princethorpe, as most locals will doubtless agree, is not a pretty one, suffering as it does by being situated where two main routes meet. However, it is fortunate in that it is surrounded by delightful Warwickshire countryside of lush fields and woodlands.

The area is dominated by the red brick tower of the Priory of St Mary, a notable landmark visible for miles. The priory was built in 1833, and was added to in 1897 by Peter Paul Pugin. Benedictine Nuns forced to flee from their home in Montargis during the French Revolution were greatly helped by Mrs Maria Fitzherbert, 'wife' of the Prince Regent, later George IV. The nuns settled first at Orrel Mount in Lancashire, but then decided to settle in Princethorpe and build their own priory. In latter years it has been a Catholic Boys' school.

Before the building of the priory, there does not appear to have been a religious house in the immediate area, which makes the story of the ghost nun even more extraordinary, since this obviously dates from centuries ago when, according to the available records, there were no nuns in Princethorpe. Yet many people have seen her; so many times has she appeared that locals have become quite used to her, and scarcely take any notice when she unexpectedly appears before them.

According to accounts, the manifestation happens in a stretch of woodland known as Nun's Wood. There is first the sound of voices, of men shouting, of commotion. Then the nun appears, moving swiftly and stealthily, her brown habit held in one hand to lift it off the damp grass. Armed men appear, violent men, who rush towards the nun. She stops when she sees them, and looks wildly about her. They brandish swords and muskets, and the nun is plainly frightened. She turns and begins to run in the opposite direction, but they overtake her, grab her and handle her roughly, and she falls to the ground.

The soldiers leave her there, and the scene fades. Legend has it that this scene dates from the time of religious persecution when those of the Catholic faith were so often hunted down and treated with violence. The old story is that an itinerant priest, perhaps one of those who travelled between the houses of Catholic families, and administered the forbidden mass in secret chapels, made his way to Princethorpe, where he hid for several days in the heart of the woodland. During this time, the nun helped him, taking him food and water, and caring for his hurts.

But as always, someone found out and laid information, probably to curry favour with those in authority. Armed men, probably the Sheriff's men, hid in the woodland in order to catch both the priest and the nun. The nun was making her way towards where the priest lay hidden, when she caught sight of those who lay in wait. Her only thought was to save the priest, and although terrified, and knowing quite well what would happen to her, she deliberately led them away from the priest's hiding place. She could not elude them. They pursued, caught and killed her, but during that time, alerted by the cries and screams, the priest was able to make good his escape.

The nun was left, a crumpled heap upon the ground, where villagers found her much later.

This extraordinary scene has several times been witnessed. Other people have merely seen the nun, gliding quietly across the fields and entering the wood, moving with ease through the fences that now bar her way. The priest too has been seen many times, making his way through Princethorpe Wood and into Nun's Wood. He seems to always follow the same path, and general opinion has it that this is the route he took when he made his escape. Whether he got very far, or whether the armed men eventually caught up with him too, we do not know.

There is no foundation in fact for this story. There are no

records, and on the face of it, it all seems a little unlikely. But all those who have seen it cannot be wrong. The story has come down through several generations, and we all know that such dreadful things did happen when misguided people were given authority to hunt down those who chose to adhere to their own faith.

18

Acts of Violence

THROUGHOUT the centuries man has perpetrated acts of violence against his fellows, and the stories of these are to be found in every county. Warwickshire is no exception and its record is neither more nor less violent than any other place. People have killed each other for all kinds of inexplicable reasons, and some explicable ones. They have often gone undiscovered and unpunished, having adroitly managed to evade what little law enforcement there was in wild and isolated places a few centuries ago. These murderous acts have often left 'something' behind them; a 'presence', an uncomfortable feeling, or an eerie chill. Details of who murdered who, why and when have been lost long ago, but the fragments of the stories remain.

Just such a story is attached to Studley Castle, off the road which runs between Alcester and Birmingham. In fact, it is not a castle at all, but a large Gothic edifice built in 1834, which its owner chose to call Studley Castle. Locals called it 'New Castle'. It has not been a family home since the end of the last century, and it was for many years a college, founded by Frances, Countess of Warwick, to instruct women in 'the higher branches of agriculture'. This venture folded for lack of funds, and since then the castle has been used for a variety of commercial training projects.

Staff employed there at divers periods have talked of the ghost and the chill feeling emanating from it, but no one seems to know much about it, except for an old story concerning a wife and a jealous husband. As in all such stories, the wife was young and attractive, and the couple had an infant son. The husband returned home one day in an evil temper, and quite without foundation, accused his wife of being unfaithful to him. The wife was horrified that he could think such a thing of her, and they quarrelled bitterly. In a fit of ungovernable rage, the husband picked up the child from his cradle and hurled him to his death through an open window. The mother, mad with grief and terror, rushed downstairs and out of the house, where she found the lifeless body of her baby, dead by his father's hand. Clutching the child's body, she ran into the woods and drowned herself in a pool there. Her presence is said to haunt the site of the pool, sobbing for the death of her babe. It has not been possible to trace the date of this story, or the names of those concerned.

Another untraceable murder has left a slightly troublesome ghost at the White Swan Hotel, Henley-in-Arden. Guests have reported nocturnal disturbances, footsteps and bumps. After a while, largely out of curiosity, the management called in a ghost hunter to spend a night or two in the haunted room to see if he could come up with an explanation, and he did! He said the ghost was that of a murdered girl, 18 year old Virginia Black, daughter of the landlord of the inn more than a century ago. She is described as clad in white, with long auburn hair, and upon her face a piteous expression. The legend is that she was in love with a man called Henry Beckett, a farm labourer, and they were to be married. One night in the summer of 1845, they had a lover's tiff which got out of hand. Henry Beckett lost his temper and pushed Virginia, but he, being a bit on the sturdy side, pushed too hard and the girl fell down the stairs. At the sight of her crumpled body lying there unmoving, Beckett became terrified at what he had done, and fled. Virginia came to her senses, and painfully dragged herself back up the stairs to breathe her last on the threshold of the room she now haunts. Beckett is supposed to have been caught and hanged for his crime.

I can find no trace of any trial or any hanging, nor any

newspaper reports of this tragedy. But that is not to say it never happened.

The pretty village of Offchurch, just off the Fosse Way, takes its name from Offa, the powerful king of the Mercians in the 8th century, who had a hunting lodge here. Offa's son, Fremund, was a young man renowned far and wide for his piety and holiness, but the King, his father, had many enemies. On his way to join his father at Offchurch, Fremund was waylaid and brutally murdered. His father had his body brought to Offchurch for burial, and legend has it that from within his tomb Fremund's pious spirit wrought many healing miracles. These apparently ceased when his body was removed, many years later, and taken to a grander resting place at Dunstable.

Here at Offchurch too, around the church itself, lingers the ghost of a man stabbed to death in the 17th century. His assailant ran into the church, sought sanctuary within the tower, and escaped under cover of darkness. The victim still searches for him in vain.

Maxstoke Castle in the north of the county has its origins at least as far back as the 12th century, and its occupants have been involved in most of the colourful events in the history of England. With all this then, one would expect to find ghost legends, but the only eerie presence that lingers at Maxstoke is upon the great staircase, where legend has it that centuries ago a son of the house murdered his brother. No one knows who, why or when, except that sometimes at midnight the door flies open, just as it did when the murderer fled.

An old house, formerly an inn, at Kenilworth has ghostly footsteps in the attic, and here there is a legend of a serving maid, murdered in the 15th century. The stories of servant girls who met their death by violence are legion, and turn up in every century, giving rise to the thought that regular employment in service was not always as safe as it sounded.

19

The Footsteps at Coughton Court

COUGHTON Court, the home of the Throckmorton family for more than five centuries, lies on the outskirts of what used to be the old Forest of Arden, about two miles from the town of Alcester. The present house was begun in the 16th century by Sir George Throckmorton, to replace an earlier dwelling. Each subsequent owner has made alterations after the fashion of his time, and during the Civil War it was three times set on fire, and later attacked by a Puritan mob from Alcester. The court is haunted by ghostly footsteps, hurrying down the staircase and causing a distinct change in the temperature.

The house is full of 'mysteries' and has been associated from time to time with various plots. The Throckmorton name looms large in English history, but perhaps the best known conspiracy which involved the Throckmortons was the Gunpowder Plot of November 1605. Sir Robert Throckmorton's daughter, Anne, was the mother of Robert Catesby, the chief conspirator in this ill-conceived plan to blow up the King and the Parliament. Another daughter, Muriel, was married to Sir Thomas Tresham who, it is believed, turned traitor and laid information which led to the plot being foiled. Another daughter was the wife of Sir Everard Digby.

Thomas Throckmorton was prudently absent from his home at Coughton Court in November 1605. He had already been in enough trouble for his adherence to the Catholic faith. Whether he knew or was involved in the plot is not known, but he did allow his brother-in-law Sir Everard Digby to take over Coughton Court from mid October of that year.

Legend has it that the ladies, together with the Jesuit fathers, Garnet and Tesimond, were sitting in the drawing room on that fateful night of 5th November. They were privy to the plot, of course. They knew Sir Everard had gone to Dunchurch, supposedly on a hunting expedition, but in reality to meet with other conspirators, and await the good news from London.

At Coughton Court the ladies sat at their sewing, although it was very late. Suddenly there was the sound of horse's hoofs, of a horse being driven hard, and Thomas Bates, Catesby's servant, hurried into the drawing room with a letter for Lady Digby. It was from her husband telling her all was lost, and to get the Jesuit fathers away if possible. What terror this news must have caused on that dark night. The ladies would have known only too well what fate awaited their husbands if they failed to escape.

Bates stopped only for a change of horses and some food, and then rode away to join his master and the others at Holbeach House just over the border in Worcestershire. Catesby was killed at Holbeach House, clasping a figure of the virgin. The ringleaders were arrested, stood trial, and later were hanged, drawn and quartered.

Tradition has it that the ghostly footsteps date from this night of fear. The direction taken by the unknown ghost is always the same; down the staircase, across the drawing room to fade away as they reach the south west turret. Could this be poor Thomas Bates still forever hurrying with the bad news? No one has yet found out.

There is another possible explanation. The Throckmortons were of the Catholic faith, and during the times of religious persecution, they had a secret chapel, and hiding places for visiting priests. Round about 1860, part of the tower chamber was opened up, and the north east turret was found to be hollow from top to bottom. Inside were discovered two ladders, still affixed together, and descending some 36 ft into a priest hole, where there was a palliasse bed and a folding leather altar. There is a legend that a secret passage exists between this priest hole and the garden, thus making it as easy as possible for a priest to make his getaway.

And then there is the staircase, brought from Harvington Hall in 1910 and installed at Coughton Court. Harvington Hall, in Worcestershire, came to the Throckmortons through marriage. It was the centre of the Catholic faith in those times when the Mass was forbidden. It was from Harvington that the Jesuit fathers Garnet, Owen, Oldcorne and Wall set out to visit their scattered flock, and returned to hide themselves in one of the eleven priest holes that have so far been discovered in Harvington.

Is it then the footsteps of some frightened priest hurrying down this familiar staircase to hide himself in some too small aperture that are heard? As a ghost hunter of many years, I believe this to be possible.

Many people have heard these mysterious footsteps, and they are recorded in many written works. They are always, apparently, heard with a sense of awe, but do not appear to have caused any fear. It is just that it would be nice to know to whom they belong.

Coughton Court was given to the National Trust in 1945, and is open to the public. It has many, many visitors, but they do not hear the footsteps. The unknown ghost walks only when the house is quiet.

20

The White Hare

THERE are many tales of hauntings at crossroads, and the reason is not hard to find, for in times long past, it was at this spot suicides were buried, usually without benefit of clergy, for the sin they had committed, that of self murder, condemned them to an unquiet grave, and put them beyond the pale of the church.

The place where two roads crossed was also where gibbets were erected so that the bodies of convicted felons could hang in their chains, and thus supposedly provide an example to all who must needs arrive at the crossroads no matter in what direction they headed. The sight of a rotting corpse was to act as a deterrent, a warning to passers-by, that here they too might end up if they involved themselves in a life of crime.

It is probable that the sight of so many hanged cadavers became somewhat commonplace, and ceased to give rise to the horror it was supposed to engender, particularly as the hanging itself was frequently gleefully witnessed by a crowd of people who made their way to the appointed place to watch the proceedings, and who bought oranges and sweetmeats from itinerent vendors and ate them while watching a fellow human being draw his last gasp.

Gibbet Hill lying between Stoneleigh and Westward Heath on the Kenilworth Road still retains its old name, and was the place where thieves and robbers were hanged. So far, they all lie quiet in their graves, except for three rascally soldiers, whose ghosts are still said to linger.

The three soldiers were dragoons from Lord Pembroke's Regiment, and they roistered and got drunk after the fashion of soldiery in 1765. Unfortunately these three carried things too far. One dark night, so the story goes, they lay in wait for three local farmers returning from market, with money in their pockets, having enjoyed a successful day of business. The dragoons planned to rob them, and viciously attacked them. Indeed, they beat all three so severely that one died the following day.

Before they could spend their ill-gotten gains, they were caught and after spending some time in gaol in Warwick, they appeared before the court there. They were sentenced to be hanged upon Gibbet Hill, the nearest convenient spot to where they committed their crime.

The whole sorry business set the local community by the ears. One of their number had been brutally killed making his peaceful way home from market, two others were injured and in any case the soldiers were invariably unwelcome interlopers, and caused much nuisance.

In the locality there lived an old woman who was reputed to be a witch and thus held in some awe. She predicted that the soldiers would not hang upon Gibbet Hill, but would be reprieved at the eleventh hour. This prediction didn't go down very well with her neighbours, who felt the dragoons had only got what they deserved. But the old woman insisted that the soldiers would stand beneath the gibbet, and as a sign that a reprieve was on its way, a white hare would appear.

All this added spice to the entire occasion, and on the day appointed for the hanging, a more than usually large crowd came from far afield to view the 'entertainment'. The soldiers were brought from Warwick by cart, and stood beneath the gibbet, their arms roped behind them. The Sheriff and his men stood ready to carry out the execution, when quite suddenly a white hare darted out from under a nearby bush and raising itself upon its back legs, it stood beneath the gibbet. This caused wild excitement among the crowd, who were then convinced that the old witch's prophesy was about to be realised. The crowd pressed forward, and the Sherriff was at a loss to know how to proceed. It was plain that if he hanged the soldiers now, he would have a riot on his hands. The soldiers began to smile, convinced their lives were about to be saved.

The Sheriff, obviously a fair-minded man, sent a messenger on horseback, posthaste, to Warwick to find out if indeed a reprieve had been granted and was at that very moment on its way. The soldiers were put back in the cart to await events, and the crowd yelled encouragement. Several of the more nimble had attempted to capture the white hare, but it proved too cunning for them, and darted off as quickly as it had appeared.

The messenger returned. There was no reprieve. How could there be? And the sentence was to be carried out in accordance with the law.

Well, the crowd had turned out to see a hanging, and that is what they saw. The three dragoons swung high on Gibbet Hill, and the white hare was not seen again.

Later the three bodies were taken down and buried beneath the gibbet upon which they had breathed their last.

The old woman had a hard time of it with her neighbours, who scorned her predictions. Some insisted that she had actually turned herself into the white hare, since it was well known that Warwickshire witches had this power.

And it is around Gibbet Hill where they died and were buried that the spectres of the three bedraggled dragoons of Pembroke's Regiment may still be seen occasionally, looking for the white hare that was supposed to herald their reprieve. Legend has it that if they find it, they will never appear again.

21

The Lillington Miser

NOT all that long ago, Lillington, on the outskirts of Royal Leamington Spa, was a quiet country village; a rural backwater, self contained, and undisturbed. Now, however, it has become more or less absorbed by the large town that is its nearest neighbour. Much of the old property has disappeared, to be replaced by a sparkling modern housing development.

Old Billy Treen's cottage has gone, long since. It used to stand on the road (then a mere muddy lane) leading to Cubbington. Slightly down-at-heel, slightly crooked, ramshackle timber and thatch, had it still been there, doubtless it would be a source of delight to those seeking the more rustic aspects of rural life in Warwickshire.

Nothing is left of Billy Treen now, except a lingering legend, and an extraordinary inscription upon his gravestone in Lillington churchyard. Do newcomers to the village read it, and wonder what lies behind it, or have they no curiosity about old Billy?

William Treen, born in 1733, was a road sweeper, and in that age when those born into poverty stayed there all their lives, old Billy presented a sad case. Little is known of his early life, largely because there could be little to know. When the stories began to grow up around him, he was simply a poor old man, living a lonely life, in his crooked little cottage that held no comfort of any kind.

He could never have earned very much, but whatever his income was, he was never seen to spend a penny of it. He scavenged for food, begging potato peelings and turnip tops from local farmers, and if they didn't give them to him willingly, he lay in wait, and took them off the top of their middens when they weren't looking. He begged too, but as always happens, everybody got just a bit tired of giving food to Billy Treen, despite his poor and downcast appearance. His neighbours probably had quite enough to do feeding themselves and their own families.

Rumours grew about Billy Treen. He never spent a penny, and he must have had a penny or two to spend! Perhaps Billy wasn't all that poor after all. It was thought that over the years, he must have managed to accumulate quite a warm little hoard. If you lived on scavenged scraps and neighbourly charity, it wasn't difficult to save your own money.

Billy himself said nothing, but kept his own counsel, and minded his own business.

By all accounts, his diet was of the poorest, and yet must have contained sufficient nourishment, for he lived to be 77 years of age, and this was quite a good life span for a poor man in those days.

He died at last in his crooked little cottage, was properly buried, and a stone was put up above his last resting place:

'I poorly Liv'd and poorly Dy'd
Poorly Bury'd and No one Cry'd'

He must have been buried 'on the parish' but who put up his stone is not on record. It sounds like the work of a local who was perhaps just a bit fed up with old Billy, or it might be that it was the sexton himself who was the rhymester. They didn't find any hidden hoard in Old Billy's cottage either, although they did look.

Time went on, and other people lived in Billy's cottage after he had finished with it. There were noises in the night, and few tenants remained long.

It was not until 1922 that it all came to light. A local newspaper carried a report that old Billy Treen's hoard had at last been discovered!

It seems that a Mr and Mrs Greenway had taken on the

tenancy of the old thatched cottage. In an interview, Mrs Greenway told the newspaper that she had never liked the place, nor had she ever felt at ease in it. She said there was an uncanny and eerie atmosphere in a room upstairs, and she had often felt quite unable to enter it. She agreed she was more susceptible to atmosphere than her husband, and she had tried very hard not to allow the feeling inside the house to upset her. But she was not happy there and felt she could not remain. It became impossible for the Greenways to use the room which seemed to be at the heart of the problem.

So much did all this upset Mrs Greenway that she and her husband looked for somewhere else to live, and eventually found another place. Before they left the thatched cottage, though, in accordance with their tenancy agreement, they had to carry out a little minor repair work in the haunted room.

Mr Greenway, doubtless being a man who could effectively carry out such small jobs, decided to do the work himself. In order to get at the back of the ceiling, he had to take out part of an ancient cupboard. You may imagine his astonishment when, tucked right down at the very back of this cupboard, his hand encountered a leather purse, damp and rotten with age. Inside the purse were silver coins dating from the late 17th century.

Until that time, the Greenways had known little or nothing of the legend of Billy Treen, 'the miserd', but locals immediately declared the coins must be the long lost hoard of this old man!

There is no evidence that this is indeed what they were, nor is there any evidence that Billy Treen did have such a hoard. Who could possibly be certain about such matters? But they must have been somebody's hoard and Billy seems the obvious candidate.

Once the coins were removed, the atmosphere in the old crooked cottage lightened, and Billy Treen's presence was not felt again. It is perhaps an even greater mystery why anyone should be content to live on charity and potato peelings while they tucked away silver coins in a cupboard to be found by some totally disinterested party more than a century later.

The cottage is no more, and the people living in pleasant modern houses built on the site where once it stood, have not noticed anything at all untoward. Apart from his cryptic gravestone, Billy Treen is no more!

22

The Unknown Ghost

CHESTERTON is a most curious place; a place where man has been, but has not lingered. Like so many other Warwickshire villages, Chesterton was depopulated and more or less deserted by the mid 15th century. Now there are only five or so dwellings, with a church at least a mile away, approached by a winding, unfenced road, with a lake on one side and fields on the other. Inside are magnificent tombs and effigies to the Peyto family, and outside, weather beaten and lopsided tombs lurch against the winds blowing across this wide open countryside. An ancient sundial tells you tersely 'See and Begone about your Business'.

Pevsner in his *'Buildings of England'* (1966) describes Chesterton as 'an eerie place which lost its heart when it lost the grand and curious mansion of the Peytos'. This grand mansion was built by Inigo Jones for Sir Edward Peyto round about 1635/40 and was said to be a rustic version of the Banqueting House in Whitehall. However, in 1802, Chesterton lost its mansion; it was completely pulled down and the building materials sold off.

Chesterton should have a ghost. It is eminently suitable for apparitions, but whether it did indeed have one is not entirely clear.

It is on record that a ghost did appear here in 1755, and talk of it stirred up the inhabitants into a state of fear. What it was, what shape it took and how it behaved itself, they did not record.

However, at that time the Rev Richard Jago held the living of Chesterton, together with that of Harbury close by. He was not only a clergyman and son of a clergyman, he was also a poet and in his day was quite highly thought of, although now his epics seem to us over-long, rather sycophantic and incredibly tedious!

He was going to have no talk of ghosts stirring up his flock, and as gossip and rumour grew apace, he decided to take action. He knew he would have a captive audience, since in those days almost all village people attended church, and he chose to deliver a stern sermon against the evils of dabbling with the supernatural.

He took as his text 'For if ye hear not Moses and the Prophets neither will ye be persuaded tho' one rose from the Dead'. He later published this great sermon in pamphlet form with the over-long title *'The causes of Impenitence considered, As Well in the Case of Extraordinary Warnings as under the General laws of Providence and Grace'*. In it he tells his congregation that those who are inclined to believe in the supernatural are called to seriousness and reformation. He belabours them about 'chambering' and wantonness, and informs them that they do not need any ghost to tell them about their bad and sinful behaviour. Whether the reputed ghost did in fact tell anyone they should repent their ways, we do not know. But Jago was obviously determined to use the possibility of this apparition to frighten his flock into impeccable and virtuous lives from now on.

He must have succeeded to some extent, for there is nothing else about this ghost on record after his sermon. Whether his flock mended their ways or simply decided they couldn't sit through any more hours of Jago's sermons, we shall never know. Or perhaps, thereafter, if they did see the ghost, they kept quiet about it.

The whole affair gave Jago another idea, though, and perhaps he didn't quite practise what he preached. Shortly after, he wrote another of his lengthy epics entitled *'Peyto's Ghost'* extending to some 15 verses, in which he purports to have been riding home to Chesterton after elections celebrations in Warwick, when he obviously thought the right candidate had won the seat. On his ride, he encountered a phantom figure who is supposed to be none other than Lord Willoughby de Broke, into whose family the Peytos married, and who was formally the owner of the 'grand and curious mansion':

'When from the jovial crowd I stole
And homeward shaped my way
And passed along by Chesterton
All at the close of Day

When through the dark and lonesome shade
Shone forth a sudden light
And soon a distinct human form
Engaged my wondering sight.'

He goes on to say how this 'human form' had eventually retired behind 'the veil of night' but not before exchanging with Jago a few patriotic and jingoistic sentiments (being also of the opinion that the right candidate had been elected), and exhorting him 'for his Country's good the solemn tale recite . . .'

The poem is intended, I believe, to poke fun at the ghost legend of Chesterton, and prevent it gaining momentum. Unless, of course, intensely patriotic and noble ghosts were the only acceptable variety.

23

The Bells of Guy's Cliffe

JUST a few miles from the county town of Warwick, in the direction of Kenilworth, is the tiny parish of Guy's Cliffe. The historian John Leland, appointed Antiquary to King Henry VIII in 1533, wrote of it as 'an abode of pleasure, a place meet for the Muses, with natural cavities, shady woods, clear crystal streams, flowering meadows and caves overgrown with mosses.' A Saxon mill once stood here, and was rebuilt in 1822. It was such a beautiful spot that it became the haunt of many artists attracted by the peaceful pastoral scene. David Cox painted it several times, and Ruskin was known to spend many hours here.

Opposite the mill is a rise known as Blacklow Hill, believed to be the site of an ancient burial ground. On top of this is a memorial stone erected in 1821 by the local Squire, Mr Bertie Greathead.

Upon the memorial stone is carved:

> 'In the hollow of this rock was beheaded on the 1st day of July 1312, by Barons as lawless as himself, Piers Gaveston, Earl of Cornwall, the minion of a hateful King, in life and death a memorable instance of misrule.'

The wording was composed by Dr Samuel Parr, the eccentric cleric of Hatton, whose scholarship is beyond repute. And yet learned persons now claim he got the date wrong, having forgotten the changes in the calendar, and that the date was in June.

Piers Gaveston was a Gascon, and the favourite of King Edward II, who heaped wealth and honours upon him. Not unnaturally, the powerful barons resented the hold the young Gascon had upon the foolish and misguided King. Gaveston was light of temperament, with a rapier wit, in great contrast to the ponderous war-like barons, who didn't understand him at all. He made fun of them, gave them all nicknames, and turned the King's face away from them. They plotted and schemed behind his back, and attempted to rid the country of him, but no matter what they did, Gaveston always bounced back.

He, it was, who nicknamed Guy, the great Earl of Warwick, 'the black dog of Arden' and the Earl roundly declared that one day the young man should feel the teeth of 'the black dog'.

The barons were permanently at odds with their King, and something like a state of war ensued. Determined to get rid of the Gascon, the barons marched to Scarborough and took him prisoner, while the King was at York. They travelled back towards London, and stopped overnight at a house in Deddington, near Banbury. But the Earl of Warwick was waiting for just such an opportunity. Together with the Earls of Lancaster, Arundel and Hereford, he went to Deddington and dragging Gaveston from his refuge, they returned to Warwick. The Earl told Gaveston 'The black dog of Arden is come to keep his oath that you should one day feel his teeth.'

Under strong armed guard Gaveston was taken to Warwick Castle, and in the Great Hall was summarily tried. He pleaded for his life, and at one stage it almost seemed as if his youth (he was only 29 years old) his wit, and his undoubted charm, might win the day. But the powerful Earl of Warwick, out of his deep hatred for Gaveston, said 'You have caught the fox. If you let him go now you will have to hunt him over again.' And so they sentenced Gaveston to death.

Under cover of darkness, on that summer night, these 'lawless Barons' took Gaveston to an isolated spot, Blacklow Hill, where they cut off his head. They then carried his decapitated corpse back to the castle. Legend has it the head remained on Blacklow Hill, a thing discarded, and it was found there some time later by a wandering friar.

More than six centuries have passed since that dreadful deed, and Blacklow Hill is still haunted by it. Despite Mr Greathead's memorial which perhaps he felt might lay the ghost, the place is still said to have an eerie feeling, emanating perhaps from the great degree of hatred those lawless barons had for the Gascon.

Local people talk of the ghost procession, and many have witnessed it. They hear the sound of horses, of subdued voices, and they see the richly garbed nobles making their sombre way towards Blacklow Hill. In the centre is the flamboyantly dressed Gascon, for he loved finery. He is bound, and riding one of the fine horses, its halter held by those who guard him. Around the horse's neck is a string of silver bells, an affectation practised by Gaveston. The young man is deathly pale, and slumps in his saddle. There is now no laugh upon his lips, no more witty barbs at the barons' expense, for he knows this is his last ride, and nothing can save him from these men who hate him.

Slowly up the knoll the procession wends its way, silent now, except for the tinkling of the silver bells, borne on the breath of the summer night.

Local people say that even if you do not actually see the procession, you can often hear the silver bells, such gentle music to accompany a deed so evil, that happened so long ago on the grassy top of Blacklow Hill.

24

Charlotte's Ghost

It is a very sad and lonely ghost that haunts Bilton Hall, near Rugby, although this kindly elderly lady does not move furniture around, or make noises in the night. She is just simply 'there'.

Bilton Hall was the home of Joseph Addison, who was born in 1672, the eldest son of a parson, in Wiltshire. He showed great scholastic abilities at an early age and was fortunate enough to receive an excellent education. His literary career began in 1693 with a poetical address to Dryden, and he followed this with his *'Account of the Greatest English Poets; Letter to Lord Halifax;* and later his opera *Rosamond,* and numerous other prestigious works. His literary output was phenomenal, and he early developed a lasting friendship with Jonathan Swift. His friend Sir Richard Steele, whom he had known since their time together at Charterhouse, founded the *Tatler* in 1709, and Addison was a regular contributor. They joined forces in founding the *Spectator* in March 1711.

By this time Addison had accumulated quite a large fortune, and he spent £10,000 on buying the somewhat decaying Bilton Hall from the Shuckburgh family, together with 1,000 acres of park land. It may be presumed that marriage was on his mind, for he began to restore the hall ready to receive his bride, Charlotte, Dowager Countess of Warwick, whom he married in 1716 when he was 44.

At Bilton Hall, Addison was able to live the quiet life of a country gentleman, busying himself with the restoration, and with laying out the gardens.

The following year, 1717, he was appointed Secretary of

State, and in this year too, his only child, a daughter, called Charlotte after her mother, was born to him. Addison was already in failing health. He suffered from asthma and dropsy, and the following March he resigned his post. He lived only one more year, dying in Kensington in 1719, and he is buried in Poets' Corner, Westminster Abbey.

His widow, Charlotte, continued to live at Bilton Hall, with her infant daughter until her death in 1731. By all accounts, they lived very quietly, and made little mark upon the neighbourhood.

After her mother's death, daughter Charlotte then aged only 14, stayed on at the hall. Doubtless she must have had a governess, and someone to look out for her interests, but other than that she was alone. And she remained alone until her death at the age of 80.

A contemporary writer said of her that she had inherited her father's prodigious memory, but none of his discriminating powers of understanding. So good was her memory that she could 'go on with or repeat the whole of' any of her father's many works, but was not herself capable of speaking or writing an intelligible sentence of her own.

Poor Charlotte, born late in life to parents who in those days would have been considered quite middle aged; the only child of a father of recognised brilliance, whom she was unable to emulate. She can scarcely have known him, since she was only two years old when he died, but her rather pathetic memorising of everything he wrote indicates that she must have been brought up by her mother, in her early years, to regard him with some reverence.

Charlotte had asked to be buried with her father in Westminster Abbey, but was told this would not be possible. She therefore requested burial in St Mark's Church, close to Bilton Hall, where she had herself worshipped regularly, and at midnight. Her last wishes were carried out. Upon the wall of St Mark's is a plaque: 'In Memory of Charlotte, only child of Joseph Addison Esquire, Secretary of State, and Charlotte,

Countess of Warwick, who died at Bilton Hall, AD 1797 aged 80 years'.

It is an extraordinary thing that no one knows just where Charlotte was buried. Her grave has not been found. Instead, sad Charlotte appears silently in Bilton Hall, her lonely home for her many years.

25

The Little Compton Clerics

LITTLE Compton is the southernmost village in Warwickshire, just before the boundary of Oxfordshire, and where the Cotswolds may truly be said to begin. It has a few houses, approached by tree-shaded lanes, and adjoining the ancient Church of St Denis, the lovely old Manor House once the home of Archbishop Juxon. Juxon it was who accompanied his royal master, Charles I, to the block, and who was the heartbroken witness when the King made his last farewells to his children.

After the King's death, Juxon came to live at Little Compton, to keep, as we would now say 'a low profile'. Cromwell did not pursue him other than to keep a wary eye upon him, and Juxon was left alone. He lived the life of a country gentleman, keeping his own pack of hounds that were described as the best in the country.

Deprived of his high office, he regularly visited Chastleton House some few miles off, a house of strong Royalist sympathies, there to take Divine Service using that same bible from which he had read words of comfort to his condemned King. He kept always the ring Charles I had taken off his own finger and given to him at the last, with just one word 'Remember'. He did remember, and his memories must have been painful ones, but he lived to see the monarchy restored, and Charles II made him Archbishop of Canterbury.

Little Compton Manor has been used as a business training college for some years now, but according to local report, Juxon's voice may sometimes be heard echoing along the passages at night, intoning those prayers denied to him during Cromwell's Commonwealth.

The very sad ghost of another much more minor cleric haunts the Church of St Denis, although he does not appear to bother anybody any more in death than he did in life. The story is that a young and unworldly curate came to serve at Little Compton sometime round about 1870. It was not long after this that Mr Drane became completely enamoured of a rather haughty young woman, who was not only most attractive, but had a very lovely singing voice, and often sang in church.

The diffident Mr Drane declared his love for this Miss Fielding, but she would have none of him. She came of a good family, and obviously knew what was due to her station in life. She had no intention of marrying a penniless curate.

The young curate was disconsolate at his rejection, but he might, given time, have overcome his disappointment. However, he was not given time, for shortly afterwards Miss Fielding announced her engagement to someone who must have seemed infinitely a more suitable suitor! With a singular lack of sensitivity, Miss Fielding went further. She insisted upon being married in Little Compton church, and that the marriage ceremony be performed by Mr Drane.

He had no choice in the matter really. The day dawned; the bride arrived, and Mr Drane joined the woman he loved to another man. Outside the church, he gently 'kissed the bride' and watched the happy pair on their way. He then disappeared, and was not seen again by anyone for the rest of that day.

The following morning, the parish clerk discovered the lifeless body of the unfortunate curate hanging from a bell rope in the Church of St Denis. He had hanged himself in despair.

His gentle wraith is still said to linger in the church where he took his own life.

Another, rather odd story is recorded about the church at Little Compton and I believe the same story is also told, with perhaps a little variation, about other places in England. It is supposed to have been written by John of Tynedale sometime in the 15th century, as a piece of church propaganda, but this is by no means certain.

The legend is that St Augustine, the first Archbishop of Canterbury (d.604) visited the church at Little Compton to preach, and was confronted with an extraordinary dilemma. The priest at Little Compton complained to the saint that the 'lord of the town' refused to pay his tithes. In those days a tithe was roughly a tenth of your income, and had to be paid to the church for its upkeep and for the living of the parish priest.

St Augustine confronted the lord and asked him why he was refusing to pay up. The man, not one whit abashed, replied that the land was his; he had ploughed it and sown it; he had laboured over its harvest, and he therefore didn't see why he should only have nine sheaves out of it. By his reckoning, he was perfectly entitled to keep the tenth sheaf as well!

St Augustine was very angry at this, and told the man sharply that nothing belonged to him, but all belonged to God. He threatened to excommunicate him, and going into the church he said in ringing tones 'I command that no excommunicated person be present at this Mass'. At that moment a grave inside the church yawned open and a dead man came from it, to move slowly across the church and through the door, where he waited patiently outside until the Mass was over.

Questioned by the saint, the dead man explained that he too had refused to pay his tithes, and the parish priest of his day had excommunicated him. Upon his death, therefore, he had been thrust into hell. At St Augustine's request, the dead man pointed out the grave of the parish priest who had excommunicated him, and the Saint commanded the long-dead priest to rise from the earth that covered him.

The priest, dragged back from the grave he had occupied for a century or more, told the saint that what the dead man said was quite true. His stubborn refusal to pay his dues, despite warnings over a long period of time, had led to excommunication. The dead man was distinctly agitated by all this, and begged forgiveness. So St Augustine had compassion on him, scourged him, and then granted him absolution. He then gave him leave to return to the grave from whence he had emerged. His body promptly crumbled into dust, and his soul thus released, sped on its way out of hell.

Turning to the old priest who had risen from the dead at his command, St Augustine suggested that he might like to return to life, and do a bit more of the church's work. But the priest replied that he was perfectly happy and very much rested in paradise, and he had always found this world a bit of a bother. He had already done his stint, or words to that effect, and if it was all the same to the saint, he would much rather remain dead. The saint then blessed him, begged that he pray in heaven for the work of the church on earth, and allowed him to return to his grave.

The 'lord of the town' watching all this was considerably nonplussed, and realised the awesome power of the saint and his church. He had an immediate change of heart, paid up all his dues, came regularly to Mass, and was usually the first to pay his tithes thereafter.

26

Ghosts of the Borders

THE village of Ilmington, lying in the folds where the Cotswolds begin, has always been considered one of the loveliest of all Warwickshire villages. It rejoices in old stone houses, mullioned windows, wells, and wonderful gardens. The hills of Ilmington rise up to the borders of Gloucestershire, with Mickleton, Chipping Campden and Ebrington as near neighbours over the border. Ghosts, not being familiar with county boundaries, wander at will throughout the area.

The night coach of Ilmington was first recorded as having been seen by a farmer at Ebrington, who watched it disappear towards Ilmington, early one morning in the year 1780. He said it was an old fashioned sombre-looking coach, drawn by six black horses, and it went at a great pace where 'mortal Jehu ne'er might drive' right over the brow of the steepest part of the hill. Had it been a 'mortal' coach it must needs have smashed itself to smithereens. There are many accounts of this night coach, some sightings on the hills, others within the village, and it has even been seen hurtling rapidly down Pig Lane.

Legend has linked this apparition with two men, one living in Ilmington and the other, his neighbour, just over the border. Somewhere around the year 1750 Mr Canning who lived at Foxcote, Ilmington, was at loggerheads with his neighbour, Captain Barnsley, whose property abutted Foxcote. The two men quarrelled over many things, and their latest altercation was about which of them had the most game on their estates. They challenged each other to a duel to settle all their issues, and the date was fixed. But immediately prior to their dawn rendezvous, they met by chance as each was walking his own boundary. Another violent quarrel broke out. Canning, enraged, lifted the stout stick he carried and attacked Barnsley, who fell dead to the ground. Canning was forced to flee the country to escape justice.

However, there were those who insisted that he did not actually flee, but only let it be thought he had, and instead he spent the rest of his life hidden at Foxcote, cared for by his family and his servants. Late at night, under cover of darkness, he would venture forth for an airing in his coach, drawn by six black horses! And he, it is, who still takes the air on the hills of Ilmington.

On the other hand, there are those who believe Canning did fly for his life, and spent the rest of his years in exile. They say the nocturnal coach actually contains the ghost of the murdered Captain Barnsley who has ever since been searching for his adversary to wreak vengeance upon him.

Another bothersome ghost was nicknamed the Mickleton Hooter, or the 'Belhowja' which made a great noise around these hills until it was supposedly laid at last. The origin of this is vested in Sir Edward Greville who owned much land in these parts in the 16th century. He had an only son, and one night, quite by accident, Sir Edward shot the boy dead in a hollow of the hills. How such an accident happened is not recorded, although throughout their long history, the Greville family seem to have been dogged by murder, mayhem and violence. The boy's screams echoed around the hills and lasted for many centuries, although sceptics did put forth alternative and more orthodox theories for the source of the Belhowja.

These hills have their own version of 'the wild hunt' too. The huntsman in this case is thought to be the ghost of Peter de Montfort, once Lord of this Manor in medieval times. He was so obsessed with hunting that he took to the field with his own pack of harriers every day, causing consternation to the clergy when he insisted on hunting on the Sabbath. One day pressing business prevented him from hunting, and when he returned home quite late, he hastened to the enclosure to see to the welfare of his pack. They, having been incarcerated the entire day, and now ravenous, did not recognise their master, fell upon him and tore him to pieces.

He, and they, roam the hills, and should you meet them, you are advised to turn away, for if your eye meets that of the huntsman, you will be forever in his power. Should he issue a command, such as the opening of a gate, you must never obey, for if you do, you will be transfixed.

According to a very strange story, all these ghosts were effectively laid to rest sometime during the last century. Hidcote, with its internationally famous gardens, lies just over the hill from Ilmington. Its beautiful house was built by the Keyte family, and in the mid 1800s was let out to a rather odd stranger called Staunton.

No one knew who he was, nor where he came from, but he was quiet enough, if somewhat unsociable, and he gave no trouble. His servants, whom he treated well, gossiped to the locals that their master spent much of his time in chemical experiments. As he was thought a kindly man, they were of the opinion that these experiments were more of a healing nature than any dabbling in the black arts. In no time at all, everyone was quite convinced that Staunton was a very clever wizard.

A group of locals approached him, and told him of their primitive fears, of the night coach, the wild hunt and the bothersome Belhowja, explaining that because of these, they could not leave their homes after dark. They said they knew he was a wizard, and would he please be good enough to rid them of these troublesome apparitions. This Staunton agreed to do. And they say he did! But he never told anyone how he did it.

A malevolent ghost is said to haunt Bruton crossroads in Ilmington, and she has been a nuisance for years. There was once a small mound marking the grave of a notorious witch here, but despite all efforts, they couldn't make her lie quiet in it.

Like most rustic witches, when she was alive her powers seem to have been largely of a domestic nature in that she could blight crops, turn milk sour, cause wells to run dry and stop bread from rising. But her greatest power was over horses. She was in the habit of waiting at the crossroads to catch farmers returning from market, when she would cause their horses to stop, immobilising them so that they could not move a muscle. She held them thus while their riders got cold or wet or both, and only when they gave her a coin, would she remove her spell and allow them to continue on their homeward way.

But the crunch came when she went too far, and was accused of causing the death of a village woman against whom she was known to hold a grudge. This woman fell ill, and her husband, a farmer, had to ride to Stratford-upon-Avon to fetch medicine for her. When he reached Bruton crossroads, the bottle of medicine clutched in his hand, the witch stopped him, and when he refused to hand over a coin, the bottle of medicine fell inexplicably to the ground, where it smashed, the precious fluid seeping away into the earth. The farmer turned around, and rode all the way back to Stratford-upon-Avon to get another bottle, but again, exactly the same thing happened. By the time he actually got home to his sick wife, the poor woman had breathed her last.

This caused much anger in the neighbourhood, and the locals banded together to hunt the witch. They decided enough was enough, and when they caught her, they hanged her at the crossroads. Her body was gibbeted there for all to see, and when a suitable time had elapsed, it was taken down, and buried at the same spot, with a stake through the heart to anchor her evil spirit so that she could cause no more trouble to them.

Only apparently the stake did not entirely do the trick, for the ghost of the old witch hung about the crossroads for many years after, and according to local report, farmers returning home from market, still had difficulty in getting their nags to move on past this accursed place.

A much more gentle ghost that nobody has ever seemed to mind at all, is that of Edmund Golding, who died in 1793, having served Ilmington's Church of St Mary as parson's clerk for many years. He is said to have loved his church and his native village so much that even in death he had no wish to leave it. He is buried in the churchyard, but his wraith is sometimes to be seen wandering about the church he cared for so much, still muttering the same responses, just as he used to do in life.

The inhabitants of Ilmington always know, though, when there are ghosts abroad, for their church bells ring, even though there are no human hands upon the bell ropes. Then, they say, you should remain indoors, for the Devil is abroad, claiming his own.

27

Inadmissible Evidence

IN the last century, almost anywhere in England, market day was the highlight of the week. Not only did farmers and their wives go to their nearest market to sell their own produce, or to buy a good cow from some other farmer, they went to meet with neighbours, to gossip, to keep abreast of events and prices. Perhaps to buy the one newspaper they allowed themselves, since newspapers were comparatively expensive in those days, and the day certainly included a good dinner with good ale at one of the local taverns.

Few farmers missed market day, and seemed to manage perfectly well without invoices and receipts, deals mostly being clinched with a formal slap of hands.

The town of Southam had a good market, very well attended by people from quite far afield. In 1820 it was very flourishing, and it was not until some 50 years later that it began to decline when local landowners would not agree to a railway link, and the town was thus bypassed. Farmers then took their cattle to Rugby where there was an important rail link, and Southam market eventually petered out.

Our story concerns a very unfortunate farmer, a regular attender at Southam market, and in a fairly prosperous way of business. For him, and most times for his wife too, market day was their 'day out' but on this particular excursion in the spring of the year 1820, the farmer went to market on his own, leaving his wife at home.

She became a little concerned when he did not turn up at the time she expected him, but was not unduly alarmed. Many farmers ended their market day just a trifle the worse for wear, and relied upon their old nag or trusty cob to get them home.

She assumed he had met up with friends, and would turn up eventually. But he did not, and when morning came she was very alarmed indeed.

She was about to set off to look for him, and doubtless give him a bit of a 'tongue wagging' when there came a knock upon the door. A stranger stood upon the threshold, a man whom she had never seen before. He told her he had news of her husband, very bad news. He had himself been to Southam market on the previous day, and had been trudging his way homewards towards evening when suddenly, out of the darkness, a dreadful apparition appeared before him. He had been very frightened, but he recognised the ghost as that of her husband, the farmer.

The body of the spectre was covered in bloody stab wounds, and its face was fearsome to behold. It groaned piteously, and had told him, the stranger, that the wounds were inflicted by a local man, Peter Thomas, who had been lying in wait as the farmer made his way home from the market. Thomas had jumped out at him, knocked him down, robbed him, and then stabbed him to death. He had then flung the body into a marl pit and the knife along with it, before running off home, his hands still bloodied from his dreadful crime.

The talkative ghost had then taken the stranger by the hand, and shown him the marl pit wherein it declared its earthly body lay. It had begged the stranger to visit his home, and tell his wife of the dire fate that had befallen her husband, and to see that the man responsible for this, the luckless Peter Thomas, was apprehended.

The horrified farmer's wife raised the alarm, and called for help from her neighbours. Together, guided by the stranger, they went to the marl pit where sure enough they found the farmer's murdered body, just as the ghost is supposed to have indicated.

Immediately, the named man, Peter Thomas, was arrested and flung into gaol in Warwick to await trial at the next Assizes.

The day appointed for the trial dawned at last, and

fortunately for Peter Thomas, it was presided over by a man of some perspicacity, Lord Chief Justice Raymond, who heard the stranger's story with some scepticism. He then ruled that the evidence of the ghost was 'hearsay' and therefore not admissible in a court of law, unless the ghost could be persuaded to enter the witness box to give such evidence 'in person'.

Accordingly, the court usher solemnly called the ghost, three times, as required by the law. The court waited. The ghost did not appear. No one was surprised, since ghosts do not usually come when called!

Lord Chief Justice Raymond looked at the frightened Peter Thomas in the dock before him. Thomas had declared himself to be totally innocent of the crime. He was a man of excellent reputation; he had no debts, and an investigation into his background had revealed nothing but his good character, blameless living and good will towards his friends and neighbours.

The Lord Chief Justice dismissed the case against him, and ordered the stranger to be detained in his stead. This proved too much for the stranger, who had tried to be just that bit too clever for his own good. He realised the game was up, and he confessed that he it was, who had waylaid, robbed and murdered the hapless farmer before throwing the body into the marl pit. He had conceived the foolish story about the apparition in order to point the finger at Peter Thomas.

The stranger then stood in the dock before Lord Chief Justice Raymond. He was sentenced to death, and was hanged in Warwick shortly afterwards.

28

The Lights of Burton Dassett

THE bare windswept hills of Burton Dassett were once lonely and bleak; a place where Iron Age man made his home, and faint traces of his encampments may still be discerned. Such a barren place was an obvious haunt for thieves, robbers and highwaymen, and upon Gallows Hill many years ago, three bodies were uncovered, thought to be those who had paid the penalty for their crime on the gibbett which once stood there.

In medieval times, Burton Dassett was far from lonely, though, for it was a prosperous settlement, well inhabited, and with a market. That is until it came into the hands of a 'wicked landlord' Sir Edward Belknap, who promptly turned all the peasants out of their homes and off the land that he might enclose it for sheep and thus become even richer. Now a Country Park, the Burton Dassett hills are home only for the sheep, rubbing uneasy shoulders with visitors who complain they are not house trained!

Strangely, with such a long and slightly murky history, it is not the wraith of a human being which has been seen flitting about these hills, but an inexplicable light.

It all came to the fore in February 1923 when, according to contemporary newspaper reports, a local man returning from his work saw a strange light upon the hills. Curious, he watched it for some time, as it flitted hither and thither, and he then saw it disappear behind the old Church of All Saints which stands quite alone, all that remains of what was once a village. The man was not in the least bit afraid, he said.

When his story got about, three other local men determined

to go out on the hills to see if they could spot the phenomenon, and indeed they did. They described it as a very strong light, absolutely dazzling, sometimes blue, mingling with red and quite beautiful in colour. It moved at great speed, but at times appeared to hover above bushes or trees, and at others seemed to lightly sweep the ground. The men said it was almost as if it was searching for something.

Many people saw this light. One man, frankly sceptical, looked at it though field glasses, and said it seemed to him to be 'reddy-blue' and 'creepy'. He said he had never seen anything like it before in his life.

A signalman working on the railway at nearby Knightcote, just north of the hills, telephoned the police and reported that the light, oval in shape, was hovering about two ft above the ground outside his signal box. However, before the police got there, it had once more floated away above the hills.

One night it spent some time hovering in the garden of a house, and the occupier reported that it had illuminated the whole house so that it was light enough to read by. A maid working at the vicarage saw it many times, as she walked back home after her afternoon off. She at first thought it was a storm lantern in the distance, but very soon realised this was not so, that it was the 'ghost' everyone was talking about. She too described it as dazzling and beautiful, and 'bobbing about' across the hills.

One motor cyclist travelling in the dark saw what he thought was like a bright star coming straight towards him down the road. He swerved to avoid it, and suddenly it had vanished.

Local people then realised that this light tended to hover above a certain wayside pool between Burton Dassett and the village of Northend. But no one could remember any legend connected with this pool which might account for it. In all the reports, those who saw this floating light said they were not in the least bit afraid of it. It appears to have caused no nervousness at all, and most of them appeared to consider it benign.

When all this was reported in the press, hundreds of the curious converged upon the Burton Hills, hoping to see what had come to be called 'the ghost', but they were out of luck. The light did not appear. Perhaps it disliked crowds.

Many learned people declared the whole thing to be silly, and suggested the light was merely marsh gas and nothing more. But this does not seem a likely explanation. All the people who saw this ghost light were local people who had lived in the area for most of their lives. They knew the hills. They knew what marsh gas was, and this wasn't it!

The ghost light flickered on and off throughout the year of 1923, and then died away. So far as I know, it has never been seen since.

29

Hauntings at Haseley

HASELEY hides itself away from the glance of the casual passer-by, amid fields and tree-lined lanes, not far from Warwick. It is a very scattered parish, with no real centre, unless you consider the church as its focal point. Haseley church, thought to be the smallest in the county, is truly a gem.

Opposite the church is Haseley Manor, a Victorian edifice in the grand style, built by Mr Alfred Hewlett, an industrialist, in about 1872. Behind it are the ruins of the old manor house built by Clement Throckmorton in 1561 to replace an earlier house, and there are traces too of the remains of a medieval village.

Like most isolated houses, and Haseley must have been a very lonely place in past centuries, the manor has many legends attached to it. One of these concerns a servant girl who is supposed to haunt the ruins, clad in grave clothes. She apparently had aspirations above her station, and was bricked-up in a secret room in the old manor house. Whether she was murdered and her body bricked-up and thus hidden successfully, no one seems to know; neither is it known who did the terrrible deed! When the building was eventually partially pulled down, sure enough a tiny bricked-up room was discovered. But there is no record of any skeleton being found within it. Nor is there any record of an underground passageway ever existing between the old manor house and the church, although there are stories that such a thing did exist, and that the ghost of the murdered servant girl uses it so that one minute she is within the ruined old manor house, and the next, on the opposite side of the road near the church.

There is a somewhat apocryphal tale that 200 years ago a

servant girl murdered a son of the house on the grand staircase in the old house. She is alleged to have waited until he came up the stairs, and then attacked him, raining blows upon his head with some kind of blunt instrument. The wall of the staircase was stained with the young man's life blood, and these stains were, like all such stains, unable to be removed. They were still being pointed out to visitors around 1900.

These legends are the kind that are oft-repeated, but the facts are completely untraceable. It may be that both servant girls are really one and the same!

The present Victorian mansion has been for many years used as a training college for the motor industry, and staff have reported vague noises, footsteps and the usual inexplicable changes of atmosphere. Tradition has it that a grey lady walks in one of the rooms, but no one knows who she might be.

There is a pool not far from the main drive leading to the house, and many locals have talked of its eerie atmosphere at night. The lamps that light this section of the drive regularly give trouble, and often fail to function properly. This pool is thought to be Fletcher's Hole, although the name has long fallen into disuse, and no one can tell me who 'Fletcher' was. As the name means literally 'a maker of bows' it may have its origins in the work of some artisan of medieval times.

Here, in Fletcher's Hole, the body of Sir Thomas de Cherlecote was found in 1263. He had been strangled by three of his servants, two men and a woman. Forensic science then being virtually unknown, it was unanimously decided that the unfortunate Sir Thomas had committed suicide by drowning himself, and the Crown wasted no time in seizing all his lands and possessions in forfeit for his crime, as was customary in such instances. His son, also Thomas, was therefore, at a stroke, rendered penniless.

However, the truth eventually came to light. How is not known, but it is more than probable that one or other of the culprits talked over their ale mugs. The three of them were caught, tried and hanged. The lands and goods so rapidly grabbed by the King, Henry III, were restored to Thomas, who had been rich, been poor, and was now rich again.

The pool is generally known as 'the haunted pool' but other than feelings of unease, and the odd behaviour of the lamps at this point, there does not appear to have been any troublesome manifestation. At least none is recorded. If there has been a sighting, then no one is admitting to having seen it. Perhaps the energy that was once Sir Thomas de Cherlecote is now finally expended.

30

The Severed Head of Astley

ON the edge of Arbury Park, the home of the Newdegate family for centuries, is the little village of Astley, in the heart of 'George Eliot country'. There are not many houses, but there is a truly magnificent church, full of interesting things, and behind it the ruins of Astley Castle present a stark and jagged silhouette against the sky line. Here in this out-of-the-way place once lived two of England's most tragic queens.

Elizabeth Woodville spent the impoverished years of her widowhood at Astley after her first husband, Sir John Grey, was killed at the Battle of St Albans in 1461, leaving her with two small sons. His estates were seized by the Crown and when Elizabeth pleaded with the King, Edward IV, for their return, he fell in love with her and married her. She became the mother of the little princes in the Tower. After her death in 1492 she was buried at Windsor, and her shade does not linger at Astley.

But it is said that Lady Jane Grey, the sad 'Nine Days Queen' does! Astley was her childhood home, and here she was happy with her books and her devotions, until her over-ambitious father, Henry Grey, Duke of Suffolk, married her against her will to Guildford Dudley, son of the Duke of Northumberland. Upon the death of the sickly 15 year old King Edward VI, Suffolk declared his daughter, Jane, Queen of England, through her descent from Mary, younger sister of King Henry VIII. Jane was but 17, pious, learned, but gentle and unworldly. She was a pawn in the power game played out by Suffolk and Northumberland.

Queen Mary, Bloody Mary, marched rapidly into London,

and threw Jane and Dudley into the Tower. They were both beheaded on Tower Hill on 12th February 1554.

'Queen Jane's Ghost' is said to have been seen flitting lightly about the ruins of Astley, the place she once held dear.

Her father, Suffolk, was also imprisoned, but was released upon the plea of his wife, cousin to Queen Mary. He got himself involved in Sir Thomas Wyatt's rebellion against the Queen, and he fled back home to Astley to hide, taking refuge in a hollow tree just south west of Astley church. One of his keepers, a man called Underwood, brought him food. But Underwood succumbed to the lure of gold, and betrayed his master when offered a substantial bribe. Suffolk was dragged from his hollow tree, and lost his head upon Tower Hill, just two weeks after his young daughter and her husband.

The actual tree no longer exists, and a stone marked the spot where once it stood, bearing this legend:

> 'On this spot formerly stood a huge hollow oak tree in which Henry Grey, Duke of Suffolk, father of Lady Jane Grey, took refuge from his pursuers. He was betrayed by his keeper Underwood and executed on Tower Hill, 12th February 1554. The tree was blown down in 1891'.

It will be noted that whoever put up this stone made a mistake in the date. The 12th February was the date of Lady Jane's execution. Her father was executed on 23rd February 1554.

The castle was later rebuilt, and much of the old building incorporated in the new, which is almost certainly why Henry Grey still haunts it. His ghost has been seen gliding soundlessly from the castle ruins to the spot where his oak tree once stood, where it disappears.

A rather macabre turn of events in this story came about in 1849 when a severed head was found in Holy Trinity church in the Minories, Coventry. This was identified, albeit not absolutely, as the head of Henry Grey, Duke of Suffolk. The skin was still intact, and the beard still retained its reddish tones. What was also evident was a certain lack of skill on the part of the headsman, for there were several deep gashes on the neck, obviously made before the final one that lopped the head from the body.

The head was exhibited in a glass case inside the church for some time, until the church itself was pulled down. What happened to this extraordinary exhibit after that I have not been able to discover. A reasonable supposition is that it was properly buried somewhere. Often when churches were either altered, restored or even demolished, this kind of thing came to light, and the usual practice was to give such gruesome remains a decent burial. The problem is that there is scarcely ever any record of where or when.

Perhaps this is why Henry Grey still flits sadly around Astley looking for his long lost head, and wondering if there will ever come a time when it may once again join his body, which would almost certainly have been buried somewhere near the place of his execution, on Tower Hill, and without benefit of clergy.

Index